The Struggle for Human Dignity

The Struggle for Human Dignity

By
Leslie E. Moser,
Ph.D.

Nash Publishing, Los Angeles

Contents

The Struggle for Human Dignity

Chapter One
Dignity and the New Humanism

A popular, if possibly inaccurate, image of the LSD user is a person abjectly staring at his hand, a leaf, or even the sun. The person, having perceptually become detached from self, turns in awe to look, shall we say, at his own hand, something that had been with him all the while but had hardly seemed worthy of attention. Yet in mind expansion, so common a thing as a hand or a leaf assumes a deep meaning and significance.

And so we get the picture. In awesome wonder, the person stares at his hand. For the first time he sees the intricate network of veins with the blood coursing through, he sees the complex bone structure, the skin texture, the creases, the lines. And he marvels. Because in the gentility of the moment, in an awakened consciousness that asks at least some of the right questions, *it is a marvel.* That which had seemed so lacking in meaning, so taken-for-granted, has finally assumed its proper importance. Here is life; and here is human; and being human is an astounding experience.

Try it yourself without LSD. Look down at your hand, think deeply, loose yourself from the pressures, the pulls of your narrow and demanding position. Look in awe at the significance of being a human.

A human being! The greatest mystery of all is man himself. The intricate nuances encased in that single phrase, "human being"—a human is *being.*

All things are being. But being a human is *something else.* When you think of it too deeply, there is always the danger that you will live with that strange and compelling reality that is the essence and meaning of life; and you may become so enthralled that you will not wish to come back to the cold reality of working, functioning, pressing, struggling—come back not to make a life, but to make a living, a mark, a status, a dollar.

Yes, it's true. Too much of this type meditation might not be healthy. A steady diet of it could result in a community of apathetic people. It is entirely possible they might not have the stamina, the determination, the drive it takes to bring off a successful, viable community of persons who for the sake of survival must fight the battles of a cold, contingent world with its unyielding demands. Where there is no persistence, no compulsive striving, there can be no sustenance.

No, a steady diet of thinking and marveling about one's humanness would not be beneficial. We must instead make do with an occasional heady diet, a quick glance now and then into the great macrocosm and the compelling microcosms of existence, a quiet time for contemplation on the things of deepest ultimacy. And then we shall take up our burdens, giving them due attention, while back in the quiet recesses of consciousness we know that we are very special—humans in the act of being.

"And what is so great about that?" the behaviorist may ask. "You are just a man, just another organism. Oh, yes, maybe with a little better and more developed brain," he'll say. But he is wrong. You are not *just* a man, at least not just any man. You must know with me that to be human is a profound experience. And being you is even more intriguing. You are a truly unique entity of flesh and blood vested with that mysterious and profound quality—existence, life itself.

Homo sapiens is the highest and most knowing of creatures. Knowing is an important part of the human situation. The human, of all the creatures, can marvel at his being and can know that behind the mystery of the blood coursing through those veins, and the existence of those bones, there are questions that will never be asked concerning not just the meaning of life, but of *human* life. Even the dormant answers to questions as yet too profound for questing speak with blaring trumpets of man's supremacy among the creatures of the earth.

If you can't feel it, I can't do anything in this writing to move you forward toward a grasp of the meaning of your life. But I hope I can move you to a confrontation with life that you have not experienced before. Life is the great gift, regardless of who or what you believe to be the giver—even if you believe there is no giver at all; and we can be partakers with the most profound sense of meaning there can be, a sense that makes us aware that human life and human living should be treated with awe and reverence. Any human life is important; you can be of magnificent importance, because you are going to know with me in the pages of this book the profundity of life itself. Together we shall glimpse the emerging, confusing, edifying, awe-inspiring unfolding of the deeper meanings of life being brought into human consciousness on the tidal crest of a surging new consciousness—the new humanism and the human potential movement.

CLASSICAL HUMANISM VERSUS THE NEW HUMANISM

Before and during the Dark Ages, there was a time in which the supernatural was pressed into service to explain everything. Man was denigrated by many cruel vexations growing out of his human nature and his human condition. Naturally, he sought comfort in explanations for his miseries. He found them in superstition, in supernaturalism, and in religion. In this era, many of the mentalisms which B.F. Skinner[1] has deplored were propounded. Man was vested with a soul, and with a capacity for faith in transcendent gods. These so-called mentalisms were necessary for survival; thus, some of them may have been foolishly conceived—*but that is no reason to believe that all were foolish.*

During the Age of Reason, man entered the period of rationalism. The philosophers of this day supposedly laid aside the products of the supernatural and agreed that man could explain all he needed to know about his existence by reasoning. Thus, the advent of classical humanism allowed no intrusion of forces outside man. Whatever god there was, was man—man was the apex of everything; he could establish a valid reason and a reasonable explanation of his existence with the power of his own intellect. There need not, so said the early humanists, be a god up there or a god out there, or a heaven above to which all "good" men might retire after life. Indeed, there need not be any immortality at all for man rationally to live his life, and in that life to achieve an important material state and a superior morality. Morality has always been an important factor in dignifying man as the highest of all creatures, deserving of kind and benevolent treatment at the hands of his fellow man. Social life and community have always been necessary in order for man to make a concerted effort to tame the brutality of a hostile nature.

As a rational approach, the Age of Reason posed a renewed emphasis on the dignity of man. It was a giant step forward. During the Dark Ages, man had largely given up his sense of dignity—his intrinsic worth and feeling of supremacy as a creature of the highest order—and instead, had concentrated his energies on visions of a hereafter. Classical humanism held that man could find his heaven now; and by giving up his opiate of a glorified hereafter, he could, with the power of his intellect, make a place of dignity for himself within a single life span and within an improved human social condition.[2]

6

THE AGE OF NATURALISM AND SCIENCE

Classical humanism has not disappeared. Indeed, some noted philosophers, psychologists, psychiatrists, etc., still hold to the classical tradition. Rollo May[3] is perhaps the best example of a modern classical humanist. With the birth of scientism and naturalism, however, there was a waning of interest in classical humanism. A skepticism began to appear concerning man's capacity to arrive at truth via rationalism. Classical humanism had placed great faith in man's mental powers, and pure rationalism was leading to the acceptance of "basic truths" because they were seen as "self-evident." But the naturalists began to suspect that under classical humanism man may have regenerated a group of mentalisms—such as free will, spirit, and soul—that were no more supportable than were the supernaturalisms of the Dark Ages. While rationalism proceeded through philosophizing about the nature of man, drawing upon so-called self-evident truths, science proposed an objective view of reality that took nothing on "faith" or self-evidence. The scientific revolution soon overpowered classical humanism.

While classical humanism was being discounted, scientism was bringing many of man's fondest hopes to fruition. Science was finding ways of conquering diseases, of filling empty stomachs, of giving man the extreme mobility of wheels and wings. Science gave man tangible fruits while classical humanism tried to give him dignity, a sense of purpose, an explanation of his being.

The age of science and technology has brought us to great heights of accomplishment. Man has walked on the moon, virtually conquered many dread diseases, and acquired not only a chicken in every pot, but two cars in every garage. But man has become dissatisfied with it all. The glories of science and of materialism cannot shield him from the uneasiness of failing to know himself; science has not been able to provide man with a quiet assurance of his own worth. As a matter of fact, technology has dehumanized, diminished, and in short, made a fool out of man. Man, who will never be content to live in some

7

utopianly biological way without seeking the mysteries of his own existence—without establishing his own dignity. There is something about man that demands a knowledge and an embracing of his own worth.

THE NEW HUMANISM

It is difficult to distinguish the new humanism from the classical. Perhaps the most valid separation is merely historical. The classical humanism came as a disenchantment with supernaturalism, with an escapist reaction to a cruel and belittling social system which placed the ultimacy of man's existence out there in a heaven to be attained after his cruel and often brutal life was past. But the old humanism could neither provide man with a solid sense of dignity nor with food for an empty stomach. It could not provide for creature comforts or for materialistic luxuries. Science and technology filled the void left by a fading classical humanism. But now, science and technology threaten a rape of the land, a destruction of the planet. The world is menaced by annihilation as a by-product of the science that spawned such promising advantages.

And so the need for a viable philosophy of life has returned in force. Most disciplines had redefined their goals with scientific stances. Scientific psychology answered many questions about behavior. But even as the hardware sciences failed to bring about materialistic utopia, behavioral sciences have failed to bring human equanimity. Skinner[4] called desperately for a technology of behavior while Maslow[5] called for a psychology of being, a third force in psychology, a new humanism.

The age-old questions of ultimacy are again being raised in a *zeitgeist* of a new humanism and a human-potential movement. Is it simply a second Age of Reason? I don't think so.

The new humanism does reaffirm the dignity of man, it does seek meaning for man's existential vacuums, it does return to the themes of man's supremacy as a creature. It seems to me, on the other hand, that the new humanism is more broadly conceived than was the classical form. The latter was reacting to supernaturalism, and would permit no intrusion of forces deemed to reside outside the organism; whereas the new humanism is reacting to a materialistic, technological society in which the human being seems to have been removed from the equation used to interpret the meaning and the meaningfulness of life. The new humanism also seems to be proceeding on two fronts.

First, the new humanism is calling for a renewal of concern for the nature of man as a creature who is biological and genetic in origin—having no claim of experience other than that vested in his organism, with environmental feedback acknowledged as very important. Still, the organism is not only supreme, it is the only supremacy, the only basis from which experience can evolve.

Yet many of the *new* humanists, as contrasted to classical, are opening their minds and their sensors to the possibility, and even the plausibility, of forces (not just environmental) that impinge from outside themselves. This new side of the new humanism is a concession to the plausibility of a "spirit world." It has attracted many followers among Christians, as well as occult groups of many descriptions including a revival of satanism. The sweeping interest in Eastern as well as Western religions and the renewal of interest in astrology testify to the extra dimension of the new humanism. This new dimension does not claim that man is the only god there is. It suggests that while man is a supreme creature, there may be explanations outside man that will help unravel the mysteries of human nature and the human situation.

Related to but certainly not always identical with the leanings of some new humanists toward spiritual resources is the emergence of a myriad of new life styles. To the critical observer, many of these life styles detract from the viability of the new humanism. They seem, while trying to promote an easy style of living, loving, and relaxed creativity, to work at cross-purposes with society.

Such life styles are best epitomized by the communes, where, for the most part, all thoughts seem centered on escaping the "system," on living close to nature, on freedom from responsibility. Such styles not only lead to a futureless, apathetic, sensually oriented people, they tend to foment criticism from those who can see no real advantage in a sell-out to a life style that promotes neither group goals nor individual responsibility. In short, hippies, communitarians, and others who opt for immediacy at the expense of an improved future are bringing unfair evaluation upon the whole of the new humanism.

Life is not, nor can it be, a constant cop-out in favor of escape from societal pressures. The future must be faced, and the future belongs to those who live with at least one eye looking forward.

As we pursue the questions and answers concerning all that man is or can be, we shall not overlook either side of the new humanism coin. More arguments will be presented in favor of man as a supreme creature, capable of dignity, freedom, and a sense of meaning within the context of his own genetic makeup and contingent experience with his environment. I also feel that the spiritual dimensions of man being coerced, directed, influenced, and molded by forces outside his own genetics and experience with his environment deserve full consideration. And, as one who does believe in a Spirit which I feel guides my life, I certainly could not belittle others who feel there are forces that impinge on their organisms.

As a psychologist, I prefer to be motivated by my own spiritual sources and resources while I offer what I consider to be a defendable position supporting man's dignity, freedom, and uniqueness within the framework of his genetics and his interaction with his tangible environment. In this sense, I believe I am meeting B.F. Skinner on a compatibly intellectual level, and playing the game by his rules. I could not counter Skinner's arguments (which is far from my full purpose here) by calling in a legion of angels, astrological inputs, or spiritual impingements of one kind or another. I am accepting, not hostile, toward transcendentalists—no matter what particular means of transcending they endorse. I simply believe that man's uniqueness, dignity, freedom, and responsibility can not only be defended against behavioristic thinking, but moved forward via a new approach to psychology within the context and the confines of a humanism. While far short of being scientific, it is, on the other hand, not supernatural.

THE SEVERAL FACES OF DIGNITY

Dignity will be the overriding concept of this effort, and should be clearly perceived in operational definition by the reader. Dignity seems to me to be an umbrella-type word that includes under its broad shadow a number of commonly understood concepts.

In the first place, the term *dignity* indicates man's intrinsic worth. One need not concede to a spiritual dimension to say that man has value because of nothing and in spite of everything. He has intrinsic value because he is human; because, for whatever reason, he is the supreme creature that possesses life and dwells on the earth. I do not say this understanding is proved or provable, only that it is reasonable.

Secondly, the term *dignity* indicates how man feels about himself. This concept is not necessarily synonymous with intrinsic worth. Man has every reason to feel his worth, his meaning, his acceptance in the universe. In speaking of man's feelings about himself, it is easily possible that a man may have dignity even if he has no intrinsic worth; or better yet, that a man may have intrinsic worth and not feel he is worthy. Man's *sense* of worth takes precedence over a philosophical concept of worth.

And thirdly, man's dignity may be looked upon as a quality residing within a given man as viewed by his contemporaries. This is an ascribed worth in which the quality of dignity may be reinforced by the approbation, the admiration, the approval of others. I consider this last concept of lesser importance; however, we cannot reasonably separate the feeling of dignity from the perceived ascription of dignifying qualities as inputs from other creatures. In this sense, the love a man feels his wife has for him, real or fictitious, ascribes to him a place of dignity;

and, if he is open and perceptive, he will *feel* dignified by such love.

THE LANGUAGE OF DIGNITY

Considering the above-stated dimensions of human dignity, the language of dignity includes many words often used as synonyms, some as determinants of the broader definition of dignity, many as descriptive of the overriding concept of man with an intrinsic value, a felt value, and an affirmed or confirmed value. We speak the language of dignity when we use words like *freedom, love, meaning, identity, wholeness, adequacy, self-esteem, morality, liberation, liberty, worth, value, concern, affirmation, acceptance,* and *received.* Conversely, we speak of dignity-robbing with words like *dehumanization, depersonalization, impersonalization, diminishing, manipulation, control, devalue, denigrate, bemean,* and *belittle.*

The dignity of man is perhaps most easily seen in the spontaneity of the child. "When we were in infancy we were able to be strong and weak, to cry when we were hurt, to weep when we were afraid, to laugh with our whole body when we were pleased. We were able to feel lovable and worthwhile, warm and wanted. Our parents were there to affirm us, to tell us that our very being as persons was sufficient reason to assure us of love."[6] In this beautiful excerpt, we can feel the reality and possibility of an unconditional acceptance of the human being. Idealistically, he can be received into a universe which gives him "unconditionally positive regard." Obviously, this is more idealism than realism as the world now stands.

The loss of dignity is perhaps most easily seen in the growing of the child from spontaneity into conformity and rigidity. "Parents and teachers took command and taught us to say 'yes' to some of our responses and 'no' to others. They taught us to live through their eyes, to hear through their ears, to respond through their own personal fears. . . . We gave adults and even siblings the right to judge our worth, to determine our merit, to manipulate our love. And in this very devastating exchange of self for a well-defined role, we lost our personality and sought constant approval from those we had given the right to define us."[7] We who are even relatively mature must know that life is never totally kind or generous. We must know that life will bring both joys and woes.[8] Human dignity asks not a bed of roses; maturity demands responsibility and capacity to face conflict.

No, we cannot remain as little children, at a stage where our dignity is perhaps most clearly defined. We must grow up and become a part of the world in which we strive for meanings—in a community of other persons who themselves are striving for meanings. But we don't have to lose dignity just because we must modify the forms in which we perceive and experience it. Human dignity is either here to stay, or human existence is in the process of disappearing forever.

Chapter Two
Recognizing the Threats to Human Dignity and Freedom

How would you react if someone approached you and asked these two disparate questions: "Do you believe you have freedom to choose which way you will go from here? Do you feel you have more dignity than your dog?"

I am convinced that most of you would respond with anger or with disgust. But there are many who believe that man has no power of choice, that he is simply a puppet pulled by his environment, his past experiences, his biology, and his genetics. We all know that some of this is true—we *are* being controlled by forces both inside and outside ourselves. Although this is not all bad—in fact, some control is necessary for living in community—most of us prefer to think that we have a choice about *most* of what happens to us.

There are many, however, who accept the concept of total control. They say man has no more dignity than a rat or a radish. Without doubt, we are living in dangerous times, and man should be aware of the forces that are challenging his right to be distinctively human—not just another animal.

The only possible way to avoid the catastrophe of human control and a sustained attack on our dignity is to become informed about these dehumanizing forces and fight back. Human dignity and the capacity for intentionality (freedom) have been the watchwords of the American dream. We will not give up this dream now!

It would be simple to say that the forces attacking human freedom and dignity are so subtle, so camouflaged that we cannot know what we should be resisting. This is not true! These ideas are not camouflaged—not any longer. Many of us have become so apathetic that we do not recognize the threats. But it is not too late to realize that we do have the power of choice, that we can become freer than we are, and above all, that we can reaffirm our dignity as human beings.

The freedom and dignity of man has been under attack since the beginning, at least since the beginning of recorded history. Imagine my excitement when after my manuscript, *The Struggle for Human Dignity,* was finished and out for publishers' review the word came: B.F. Skinner is bringing out a new book *Beyond Freedom and Dignity.*

I had considered B.F. Skinner an adversary of my system of thought for at least the twenty-odd years since his novel *Walden Two* appeared. I had alluded to *Walden Two* as well as to *Walden I* (Thoreau) in my book. But here was fresh material by a most honored challenger. I knew so well what this man had done for society in perfecting operant-conditioning techniques. I had witnessed the great successes these techniques had brought to teaching, to the treatment of the mentally ill, and to the general field of behavior modification.

Beyond Freedom and Dignity[1] was more than I had expected. I found a new dimension in B.F. Skinner. He had lost none of his scholarly mien; he stated his views sharply and incisively; his prose style was largely unchanged. But here was a different Skinner, a man with a greater intensity than I had known before, a person who had urgent and evangelical zeal about what he was saying. I thought as I read, "This is unbelievable." It is one thing to pose a proposition for the sake of scholarly debate, it is still another to perfect a "token economy" system for dealing effectively with mental retardates, but it is a frightening new development to call for a definite plan of action based on a concept of total human control. I admit I was shocked and shaken by this encounter.

Now, as I look back on this new experience with Skinner's work, I can think about it more logically. I know that B.F. Skinner is a very knowledgeable man; a person who would say only what he believes, what he thinks would help the human community achieve a better way of life. But I do not agree with what he says. I am afraid both of what he says and what he implies. I believe that all scholars are taking Dr. Skinner's remarks very seriously; and believe me, I am.

Let us take the time to look at some of the things Dr. Skinner says; and knowing that he has many followers, we shall not be guilty of belittling any of them. We must, however, think carefully in order to understand fully the threat these ideas pose to human dignity and freedom.

It is my conviction that the world needed this book. Dr. Skinner's terse suggestions have caused all of us who believe in man's freedom and dignity to look closer at our arguments and convictions. If, after reviewing them, we are not more convinced than ever of our position, then we should discard or revise our own arguments. The "Skinnerians" have a definite plan of action. They call for a crash program in behavioral technology, a program which moves from a foundation of denial of human freedom and dignity.

Dr. Skinner declares that man's behavior is determined by two factors, his genetic endowment (both in the individual and the racial sense) and his environment. It is extremely unlikely that these two determinants tell *all* about human behavior.

There is little suggestion in Skinner's book that mankind enter any sustained program to improve genetics, although many others are suggesting various ways and means of doing this through genetic surgery, parthenogenesis, and other methods of human engineering. Skinner does suggest that the human organism and his behavior must be controlled in order that man may survive on this planet.

There is no question that man has been and is being controlled. The type of control Skinner has always suggested has been control of the masses by a select elite. What seemed an exciting innovation in communal living in *Walden Two*,[2] and an intriguing issue for debate in other works, has now been suggested as a modus operandi for saving man and the planet. As Arnold Toynbee[3] has evaluated it, this gives one "an uneasy feeling of unreality."

But again, control is necessary. And few people like control. To most people, being controlled means losing freedom. But freedom is relative, and controls of some types may help us gain viable freedoms. It really does upset me, however, to hear that man has no dignity. I know that Skinner and I wouldn't define dignity the same way, but more about dignity later!

Without some manner of control, we would certainly be stepping on each other. No democratic ideal could possibly work, no American dream could come true. In *Beyond Freedom and Dignity*, Skinner says, "The problem is to free men, not from control, but from certain kinds of control."[4] I wholeheartedly agree!

Of utmost import to me is the type of controller envisioned and the way in which the controller sees those controlled. Most of us have thought about control as a democratic process in which the chief element is self-control. But now we are faced with a proposed program of control which envisions the persons controlled as creatures having no such redeeming qualities as free choice or dignity. Chaim Perelman,[5] author of *Philosophy and the Law*, finds the prospect of a "behavioral scientist's enlightened despotism" frightening.

We all knew that Skinner believes rats and pigeons have no such inner qualities as free choice and dignity; and Skinner, being an atheist, should not be expected to propose that man has a soul or a spirit. Instead of being an isolated dream, *Walden*

Two has become—in plan, at least—a national reality. Man is seen by "the controllers" as having no power of intentionality or autonomy. Possessing no capacity for making decisions except within the context of his genetics and his reinforcement contingencies, which have shaped his behavior up to the present and which will continue to shape his behavior, he must be controlled.

The controllers, strangely enough, are totally controlled, too. But they have supposedly gained a knowledge based upon their own genetics and reinforcement contingencies which will cause them to shape the environment and the humans within it in directions resulting in the common good, somehow determined (valued) by these controllers. The values to inhere in the "good society" would be arrived at by carefully monitoring various behaviors with a decision being made somehow as to which behaviors are to be positively valued in cultural survival. Harvey Wheeler[6] points out the obvious circularity of this plan. The earnest question as to what will be considered prevailing values is passed off by the Skinnerians as "some version of natural law," or as "conventional wisdom." Cultural survival is their end, and the means must somehow be determined without violating the concept of man's inability to participate in intentionality—more circularity.

So, in essence, *Beyond Freedom and Dignity* proposes the nature of man as being without the capacity of intentional acting, without inner (autonomous) resources beyond that which genetics and reinforcement contingencies have provided. It would not be so frightening if the plan were not being taken so seriously. Strangely enough, this book has become a best-seller and the proposals therein are seriously considered by literally thousands of people, although Lord Ritchie-Calder, professor at the University of Edinburgh and author of twenty-eight books, considers Skinnerians as latter-day determinists and believes their proposal to be a bleak proposition.[7]

In a recent symposium at Santa Barbara's Center for the Study of Democratic Institutions, a number of international dignitaries presented papers condemning these ideas of Skinner's. In an interview, Dr. Skinner[8] declared that he "had been misunderstood." But my reading of the interview and a rereading of his book shows me that these straightforward, difficult-to-misunderstand, sharply incisive statements actually mean to write mankind off as a creature without freedom or dignity. It is probably true that Dr. Skinner's intent was misunderstood, but his language is quite distinct. As I read *Beyond Freedom and Dignity,* I hear him saying that man's behavior is unalterably determined only by his genetics and his environment. Man has no autonomy, and he has no dignity. It is true, of course, that Dr. Skinner's use of the terms "autonomy" and "dignity" have special meanings to him, as we shall see. I feel that the Skinner who wrote *Walden Two* has mellowed to the point that his concept is now a "soft" control as opposed to those controllers in *Walden Two* who forced hungry children to stand at attention while their steaming soup became cold so as to condition them for the quality of patience.

I am convinced that Dr. Skinner means man no harm, only benevolence. That he feels this "good" may be achieved only through human and environmental control can scarcely be doubted. He constantly reaffirms it.

The Skinnerian view is that man has reached this sad state in his development—a deplorable state of technological control, pollution, and crime—because he has refused to give up his foolish notions that he has freedom and dignity. Skinner believes that only by giving in gracefully to control can the human race survive.

Since the behavior of every human is "determined by a genetic endowment traceable to the evolutionary history of the species and by the environmental circumstances to which, as an individual, he has been exposed,"[9] it follows that man—through championing the prescientific view that a person's behavior is at least to some extent his own achievement—has brought himself to the brink of disaster. What is more, Skinner argues, the only way we shall survive these crises that are upon us is to expand our behavioral technology and determine the direction man should be going in quest of a better world for all.

A reasonable proposition. Yes, if we accept either that man's prescientific view of himself has brought us to this sorry state or, on the other hand, that the scientific view will remove us from it. My own appraisal of the situation is that without man's belief in his freedom and his dignity, the world would not have survived even to the time of the building of the Great Wall in China, to the time of Christ, and certainly not through the Dark Ages. Man could not have survived without his concept of a dignified self, and he *will not survive* if he loses it. Perhaps he will not survive anyway, and he certainly cannot survive if he continues to allow his dignity to be undermined by repressive religious dogmas, technological revolutions, or affluential societies. He will definitely not survive by surrendering to elitist controllers, however intelligent, however benevolent.

I have no doubt that Dr. Skinner actually believes his system will give us a society better than the one we now have. Many people look upon Skinner's proposed society very favorably. John Platt, in his *A Revolutionary Manifesto*[10] says, "A society for survival with immediate feedback channels of protest and correction, a society that ends a long reign of punishment and retaliation . . . a society that deliberately practices diversity and experimentation with different life-styles . . . such a society looks to me not like a blueprint of hell but more like a blueprint of heaven from where we stand today." And in *Beyond Freedom and Dignity* Skinner declares, "we have the physical, biological, and behavioral technologies 'to save ourselves'; the problem is how to get people to use them."

How great this sounds! And, again, I believe that Skinner believes what he is saying and that Platt has correctly reflected what Skinner feels about the new behaviorist-controlled society. It seems clear to me that the furor over this book would not have arisen had Skinner only suggested such a control in the context of man still possessed of his freedom and his dignity. But he did not. It is the denunciation of freedom, the autonomy that belongs to a man of dignity, and the belittling of the literature of freedom and the dignity that frighten men.

21

I would have to be counted among those who believe with conviction that man has these qualities that Skinner denies, and I would say with Max Black, "A world of well-controlled bodies, emitting physical movements in response to secret reinforcement, might perhaps seem hardly worth preserving."[11] While this is a strong statement, I do not consider it harsh. On the other hand, the statement "It may, after all, be better to be dead than bred—like cattle"[12] does not sound to me like what Skinner meant to imply at all. However, I cannot with any grace surrender my rebellion at being thought of as a man without dignity or freedom.

THE QUESTION OF THE INNER MAN

In *Beyond Freedom and Dignity,* Skinner refers to "cognitive" activity in man as "perhaps the last stronghold of autonomous man. Because it is complex, it has yielded only slowly to explanation in terms of contingencies of reinforcement." Since this is a part of the overall attack on the "inner man" concept, he is saying that the inner man shrinks each time a new revelation of a former behavior is explained as a reinforcement contingency.

It is my feeling that Dr. Skinner's concept of the inner man is not at one with his concept of autonomous man. To me there are two possible concepts of the inner man. In one concept of inner man there dwells all that science has not as yet been able to find out about man; thus every time a scientific fact emerges, we take that part of man's behavior out of the "inner chamber" and place it among the "knowns."

It is my contention that Skinner's autonomous man belongs inside my inner man. If we do look at man as a creature whose behavior is so complex that it presently defies scientific inquiry, then we must admit that most of man's behavior is "inner."

The big question is whether new revelations via controlled scientific experimentation must always yield information that cuts down on the concept of man's dignity. I think not!

It would not surprise me if the inner man should continue to shrink via new understandings, hopefully to the vanishing point.

We might then understand all of man's behavior. It is my firm belief that laying man's behavior bare might well expose his capacity for intentionality and thus enhance his sense of dignity. We may find, on the other hand, that all of man is not within man; we may be forced to concede, then, that man is influenced by some form of spirit world.

Many years ago, Otto Klineberg[13] suggested that there were three tests to determine if a given quality is indeed a part of the nature of man. There would have to be continuity—evidence of possession of a trait along the phylogenetic scale; then, universality—evidence that this trait is possessed by peoples around the globe; and, finally, the acid test, some relationship to human biology. So far as intentionality and dignity are concerned, it is at least as supportable to consider these qualities a part of the nature of being human as it is to declare them not to be so.

In terms of the continuity principle, as in many matters of the "nature" question, it is just as well not to begin a search. We have no reasonable means of showing intentionality or dignity to be a part of the bird or animal world, for instance.

When it comes to the universality principle, however, we are on ground some may consider to be quite sound. For twelve years now, Lawrence Kohlberg[14] has been researching the question of universal morality. He has, within the context of a very sound research design, carried out his research around the world—in Turkey, Taiwan, Mexico, Malaysia, Yucatán, and the United States. His data show that basic moral values are universal. Regardless of culture or religious background, stages of moral development and the capacities of at least some persons in each culture to reach the more advanced stages were clearly demonstrated. True, there were cultural derivatives of the moral growth patterns; young people in the various cultures showed cultural relativity reflected in manners in which their moral valuings were expressed.

In each group studied, when the cultural development stage had moved to its highest possible levels, it was shown that a "principled morality" had developed. It was demonstrated that among all peoples studied, some persons continued to mature to the highest stage in morality wherein seemingly self-chosen, ethical principles were espoused. As Kohlberg[15] states, "At heart these are universal principles of *justice,* of the *reciprocity* and *equality* of the human *rights,* and of respect for the dignity of human beings as *individual persons.*" In other words, there is a moral imperative to value life; not just human life, although human life does seem to be more highly valued than other forms.

In a study by J. Rest[16] which dealt specifically with the question of *motives* in "moral action," it was shown that the sequence in moral-judgment growth is invariant, each stage depending on the one preceding it. It was further shown that a physiological basis for moral growth is not required in order to explain these phenomena; that is to say, no genetic component is necessarily involved.

Kohlberg and Turiel[17] have followed this with further research involving the cognitive-developmental approach, and have shown that moral development proceeds from a cognitive core, and again, that education and socialization does not transmit fixed moral values but merely stimulates the child's restructuring of his experience to activate the "cognitive core" that seems to be present in every human.

Thus, with the Kohlberg and Turiel research, the universality of moral judgments reflecting human dignity and the value of life are well demonstrated—if not with finality (few things are), then at least within a carefully controlled research design. Kohlberg and Turiel[18] do not force closure on the proposition that the highest stages of universal morality are biologically determined. They strongly suggest that the highest stages most often are emergents of social interaction. With the youngest child studied, however, there was clear evidence of basic values of human life and the capacity to empathize with others.

Does moral judgment which causes humans to see universal value in life have a physiological base? There is no reason to think that it does not. Skinner firmly argues for behavior which is two-part, brought forth from genetic endowment or from reinforcement (learning). Why should we doubt that there is a physiological structure for human intentionality (a behavioral action) which would, in turn, yield credence to human dignity (a passive state). Skinner decides that such structures are not really there, that they are a function of the mysterious (and fictitious) little man inside (inner or autonomous man). He doesn't really know what is in the inner man any more than I do. He confesses that human cognition has yielded slowly to enlightenment by supportable research which, he hopes, will eventually reveal cognition as a fully explained entity conforming to his genetic-plus-learning model.

A few years ago, Noam Chomsky[19] was caught in a similar confounding situation, feeling the necessity to explain how a child arrives so swiftly at being able to put words together to make meaning. For centuries it had been supposed that children learned to put words together in meaningful sentencelike structures because they were imitating others. But Chomsky admitted that such a feat would be totally impossible; a child could not possibly hear and imitate the thousands of combinations which seem to roll off his tongue once he has gained a certain level of language facility. So, Chomsky proposed that somewhere in the neural structure—probably in the cortex—there must be a "language acquisition device" (LAD). Some psychologists and geneticists thought that was not a reasonable explanation. They just couldn't accept the idea that there was a "device" in a child's head that caused him to "crank out" sentences.

It comes as something of a shock that psychologists have been caught on these horns for years. How to explain learning? We just have to say that it's a cortical function, as yet unexplained. Many human behaviors have been explained this way—we don't know yet, there are undoubtedly structures in the cortex that aid in cognizing, learning, motivating, etc. We haven't given them names as Chomsky did, but our explanations are just as ambiguous, just as filled with evidence of our anxieties which seem to rise when we are forced to say, "We just don't know."

The truth is, we just don't know! We don't know about intentionality, either. If and when we do find out, it is just as logical to believe that intentionality is "housed" in a cluster of cortical cells and is just as genetically biological as is learning. Skinner has been performing conditioning experiments much like the aborigine who, dipping his arrows in poison, brings down the game without knowing what is in the poison. Operant learning works beautifully; and Skinner deserves a lot of credit for making it available to us for the many projects to which it is being applied; but we don't know what causes it to happen.

CONSCIOUSNESS, AWARENESS, AND EXPERIENCE

Skinner, in *Beyond Freedom and Dignity*, admits to ". . . the indisputable fact of privacy: a small part of the universe is enclosed within a human skin." This seems to be Skinner's interpretation of what nonbehaviorists call experience. A person is conceded to have experience within this skin, and this intimately private world is contrary to a "richer form of knowing." As a matter of fact, this private world of experience is a hindrance, at least to the "process" of knowing. Skinner says, "The difficulty is that although privacy may bring the knower closer to what he knows it interferes with the process through which he comes to know anything."

On the topic of human awareness, Skinner is particularly adamant in disclaiming anything approaching Maslow's concept of peak experience, or of transcendental life or thought. He sees all consciousness as verbal. "Without the help of a verbal community all behavior would be unconscious. Consciousness is a social product. It is not only not the special field of autonomous man, it is not within the range of solitary man."

I hope I am not misunderstanding Skinner on this point. If I am understanding him, then it is clear why the humanists, the religious, the psychoanalytical, the devotees of mystical and/or spiritual existence, ad infinitum, would rebel. That they do rebel hardly shows they do not understand Skinner.

To say to a Zen master, a Christian, a humanist, or almost any man on almost any street that he cannot have consciousness without words would cause most to do a double take in slack-jawed unbelief. The unsophisticated may not rebel, because they may not fully understand the words themselves; the sophisticated nonbehaviorists (and many who think of themselves as behaviorists) would be amazed that a man of Skinner's intellect could make such a statement. Some would turn away with sadness saying, "He just hasn't had my kind of experience (consciousness)." Quite contrary to what I hear Skinner saying, I believe that words (and the verbal community), in at least many instances, are a hindrance to consciousness at the deepest level.

ON HUMAN DIGNITY AND CONSPICUOUSNESS

As I understand Skinner, his concept of human dignity is a peculiarly shallow one. He seems to equate dignity with the amount of credit a man receives from his fellows (the third dimension of dignity proposed in Chapter One). Thus, his dignity is ascribed to man by man, and is not at all intrinsic. Man, therefore, must earn his dignity. But he cannot really earn it, because he does not really have autonomy. He can only pretend that what comes forth from him (words, deeds, altruisms, etc.) are coming from inner resources—the little man inside the big man. So, essentially, Skinner's concept of dignity is a quality which is foolishly and erroneously ascribed to man by men. His declaration is that dignity doesn't exist.

To those of us who believe in the intrinsic value of life and the intrinsic worth of the individual, this view of dignity is despairingly shallow. But if we saw dignity that way, we would probably say with Skinner that man has no dignity. This is a point wherein it would be easy to misunderstand Skinner. It is not that Skinner is trying to do away with man's dignity in some demoniacal show of superior wisdom; he simply doesn't believe in dignity as a plausible concept except in his ascribed sense. A person who has the view of man that Skinner espouses couldn't possibly and with honesty believe that man has dignity.

But with Kohlberg's research on universal values of human life, those who have accepted man's intrinsic worth on faith may continue to do just that. And with that we can very well be content. For those who believe in man either as spirit or as having an indwelling, there is no problem; and it shouldn't make any difference what Skinner thinks. For those who would be happier with a less ephemeral explanation of dignity than the spiritual one, there is the Kohlberg research as a point of departure.

If man by nature (possibly by genetics) does supremely value human life, then he affirms each human. Thus man has dignity not as an ascribed virtue, but as a function of his humanity. He has being, he is being-in-becoming; and his fellowmen value his being-in-becoming, his being-in-growth.

Chapter Three

The Emerging
New Psychology

Psychology as a science is said to have begun in Wundt's laboratory in Leipzig about 1879. This confirmed an abrupt departure from "armchair philosophy," which derived its truths from pronouncements of supposedly wise men. In an effort to bring psychology into a scientific posture, Wundt and his followers began to emulate the physical sciences, which were thought to espouse the only creditable format for science. In the physical sciences the format included experimentation and operationism. Concepts were to clearly defined; and the procedures by which these concepts were to be measured empirically had to be sharply specified. Variables that might possibly affect the experimentation had to be controlled.

As might have been expected, Wundt and his immediate followers failed to handle the task, principally because they started dealing with conscious experience via self-reported feedback from the subjects themselves. These efforts quickly faded into disrepute.

Freud was the next sage on the scene. In spite of the superiority of Freud's intellect and the astuteness of his clinical judgments, his theories concerning human behavior could not be tested experimentally—psychoanalysis never really claimed to be a science. In America, during the early part of the twentieth century, McDougall began to list human instincts. It became quite a game; but again, the instinct theories could not be put to experimental test.

THE RISE AND IMPACT OF BEHAVIORISM

The next major movement in psychology was behaviorism. This started in Russia with Pavlov's conditioning experiments. These experiments, moving out of a matrix of basic biological urges and conditioning techniques designed to shape behavior through tension-reduction, were picked up in America by John B. Watson. The heralded science of behaviorism has been the principal watchword in American scientific psychology since that time.

Scientific behaviorism has flourished in America, since such a sweeping theory could be used to explain almost anything. The basic needs of man were seen to be biological, and by utilizing these needs and by shaping behavior through proper reinforcement, almost anything could be made to happen—or any behavior could be explained if it did happen. Under the behavioristic umbrella, a man could become a powerful financial success or President of the United States. Everything was possible, given a favorable genetics and cleverly planned or favorable happenstance reinforcers. And it all came about because man had identifiable biological needs which could be manipulated in almost any way imaginable through reinforcement toward tension-reduction. It all fit together very neatly.

Social psychologists began to be affirmed in their study of social processes. Man by nature was only biological, but he did live in a social context. Hence, it was acceptable science to study emergent social features so long as it was conceded that these social realities proceeded out of the basic biological needs which, being reinforced in various ways, caused behavioral variants in the many human societies. Within behavioristic thought, these social qualities in man were simply offshoots of man's basic biological nature. As such, they too deserved scientific attention so long as social scientists never forgot that the society was shaping the man by reinforcement contingencies. Man was never allowed, in this format, to be by nature anything but biological. If he loved another or if he himself seemed to crave affection, it was only because his behavior had been shaped this way from the matrix of biological needs and tension-reduction via reinforcement.

It must be said here that not all scientific psychologists are classical behaviorists or necessarily behavioristic in their outlook. For many researchers, the field of inquiry does not dictate a stand that would label them one way or another. Still, from roughly 1925 until about 1960, scientific behaviorism after Pavlov, Watson, and Skinner was a principal, if not *the* principal, matrix of psychological thought.

Clinical psychology adopted a scientific-professional model soon after World War II. Within this model, the practitioner deals with clients by utilizing information gathered by scientific psychologists; he endeavors to understand his clients at least partially through research findings. Since about 1960, there has been a strong movement toward the acceptance of behavior therapy and behavior modification. These practitioners make the research findings of scientific psychology available to their clients; thus bringing about changes in behavior which for the most part are agreed upon by the clients themselves. At any rate, many behavior-modification proponents do not accept the narrow dictum of the classical behaviorists that man's behavior comes only from physiological needs and reinforcement contingencies. There is clear evidence that behavior modifiers are moving forward with a technique-orientation as opposed to a research-theoretical-orientation.[1]

In my first contact with psychology as an undergraduate student, it was suggested to me that psychology should attempt to understand, predict, and control behavior—in that order. It is now my belief that this order is of necessity being reversed, and man must be controlled, *in some special cases,* before he is understood. Considering the state of the world, I can certainly concede that under certain circumstances it must be this way. I do not believe, though, that we should give up trying to *understand* human behavior, nor do I believe we shall ever succeed in understanding through the behavioristic model.

Since psychology is admittedly a very complex study, there has always been a strong plea for an economy of ideas. In a way, classical behaviorism accomplished this by asserting that physiological drives and reinforcement contingencies are the "be all and end all" of human behavior.

THE WANING OF BEHAVIORISM

It is too good to be true. And, obviously, it isn't the whole truth. In 1959, R. W. White[2] pieced together an impressive array of insights which emerged from a combination of disenchantment with Freudianism by the neo-Freudians and with behaviorism by the neobehaviorists. White's article, "Motivation Reconsidered: The Concept of Competence," was an important milestone in the continuing disenchantment with scientific behaviorism, especially within the classic style provided by Pavlov, Watson, and Skinner.

The neobehaviorists had begun to see, even in their laboratories, that neither animals nor men are by nature totally and exclusively driven by tissue needs. For example, Olds and Milner[3] demonstrated that animals in a Skinner box would work themselves to near exhaustion just to experience a seemingly pleasant charge of electricity through an implanted electrode to a specific section of the brain.

R. W. White continues to argue that the tension-reduction model based solely on physiological needs does not explain either animal or human behavior very well. White's model, given under the label of "competence," shows that men and animals seem driven by more cognitive conditions. He says they seem to possess at an early age such needs as curiosity, novelty, mastery, and manipulation. Although White stops short of declaring these needs innate, he does challenge us to watch the behavior of young children. Without having had the opportunity to learn these needs, they respond universally to these needs; it is enough to make any reasonable person suspicious of the idea that only traditionally defined biological drives are innate. Etzioni[4] argues strongly in favor of "basic human needs" for affection and recognition. I believe we are on the threshold of a new era in psychology, an era in which many aspects of typical human behavior heretofore considered acquired will be recognized as genetic.

It seems to some of us that disclaiming these virtually self-evident truths about human behavior while trying to *understand* behavior toward the ultimate end of benevolent control is a futile exercise. Why not consider that human beings have innate needs for affection and for recognition, for instance, even though there is no *apparent* biological basis for these needs. After all, why must innate needs always have biological bases as traditionally defined? Why not accept the seemingly evident (even if ultimately it might be "proved" to be otherwise) and move from "reasonable" positions toward "reasonable" understanding? Why not accept that the human being needs affection until it is proved otherwise?

Behavioristic psychologists seem to be a bit headstrong. In the face of scientifically derived evidence that man has some nonbiological needs, behaviorists persist in believing that these qualities are acquired drives. For many, these qualities must be proved beyond *any* doubt before they will include them in research designs. For others, it is not likely that the existence of nonbiological needs will ever be so proved, because they steadfastly refuse to believe it.

As I see it, it is time for scientific psychologists who hold to the behaviorist model to give up the idea that nonbiological qualities must be kept out of their experimental designs. By refusing to concede even to the *possibilities* of these needs and this newly reaffirmed concept of the nature of man, the behaviorists are blocking out the possibilities of *ever* understanding man. Behaviorists stand now analogously where therapists once stood, disclaiming any moral (value) orientation for their "treatment." Most, if not all, psychological practitioners have given up an amoral therapy; and it is time for scientists to give up the idea of a human nature defined only by biological needs. Only by accepting the broader spectrum of basic needs for the human can scientific psychologists ever hope to understand man. In the meantime, further research that denies these innate qualities is becoming less and less productive; and many psychologists are capitulating to the proposition that man must become controlled even without his consent. And, indeed, he must be in many cases. But man can be minimally controlled while maximal effort is made (through an enlarged concept of the nature of man) to understand him.

AN ENLARGED GENETICS RESHAPES PSYCHOLOGY

Skinner[5] has proposed that man's behavior is a product of his genetics and his environment. This may be entirely correct. The trouble is, as I see it, that Skinner's concept of the genetic is extremely limited. His narrow viewpoint is the epitome of the fading acquiesence to genetics as comprised of physiological needs and physical structures, speaking both in terms of racial and of individual heredity.

It seems to me that a new concept of genetics is upon us. Perhaps this new era was ushered in by Watson and Crick with their discovery of the DNA molecule and all the continuing emergents from this event. The concept of the computer may help us in our search for the totality of the new genetics. It has always been apparent that within the human cell there was a "program," a program which would operate to produce a kidney in the human fetus that would be in shape and function just what human kidneys have always been. Similarly, it is probable that there are programs in the human cells which dictate the brain structures from which emanate the capacity to learn. Human genetics, especially, is now being seen as a much more complex and a far more encompassing cause of behavior than before.

There is no doubt that psychologists in general are intuitively accepting the idea that the human is genetically a creature of many programmed structures which produce many behaviors. Psychologists are also seeing that these behaviors are not dictated *in toto* by reinforcements made by the environment upon the basic needs systems (as traditionally defined) of organisms. In short, psychologists are ready to accept a greatly expanded genetics concept for all organisms. For example, almost every psychologist accepts the Piagetian phases of cognitive development. The fact that these stages occur in the *same* sequence in *every* child regardless of social situations or any type of conditioning procedures is testimony of the reality that through genetic endowments, there are structures (probably neurological) which predispose the child to eventful behavior largely unrelated to reinforcement contingencies. The child experiences these stages because his genetics dictate that he have them.

We are at that point in scientific psychology now when it is ridiculous to hold onto antiquated notions of the preponderant effects of reinforcement contingencies upon behavior. Certainly reinforcement shapes behavior. But much of the behavior we had earlier thought to be learned is now highly suspect as not being caused only by learning. More and more we are seeing that an organism's genetics can be extremely far-reaching.

Is there a genetic explanation of the seemingly universal need for affection? Is there a genetic explanation of the seemingly universal tendency to value life? The answer to these questions is very probably yes. And where does that leave scientific psychology? In one sense, psychology is left in the very unenviable position of having had its vitals torn from it. At best, psychology as a science is struggling for a new identity. But that identity can never come for any of us so long as we continue to hold onto that which is no longer viable. We reasonably know that many of the things we had earlier ascribed to learning are at least aided by genetic programming; that is, learning is not the entire answer. Our best hope is to move toward research that will explore and explain all that man is by virtue of his genetics rather than hiding behind no-longer-defendable claims that man's behavior can be explained by understanding the reinforcements of physiological drives. No science has gained by avoiding the issues; and psychology is faced with the obligation of denying the error of its ways as regards scientific behaviorism.

NEW ROLES AND IDENTITIES FOR PSYCHOLOGISTS

Our position now is not an enviable one. We must hold many things in abeyance while the new genetics is being explored. It is difficult to say how psychologists, locked in as they seem to be by methodologies that were created to serve fictitious concepts, may become involved with the task of enlarging understandings of the new genetics. It is obvious that understanding genetics is largely within the purview of microbiologists. Psychologists need to seek rapprochement with microbiologists in order to lend support and energies to the search for the realities of a broadened genetics concept. No psychologist sees very favorably the prospect of waiting while someone (some other professional group) provides understandings upon which we may reasonably base a renewed search for understanding behavior. Psychologists are moving swiftly in order to be a part of such a search.

But beyond waiting for new information on genetics and/or helping in the quest for this information, psychologists may accept highly probable indicators, and treating them as "tenable fact" may press their search concurrently with other searches for other understandings from other disciplines. Again, why wait until it is proved beyond a doubt that a part of man's racial inheritance is a need for affection? Every scientific endeavor moves ahead on assumption. Behaviorism occupied the forefront in psychology for nearly half a century with faulty assumptions. The emerging new psychology should accept "low risk" assumptions and proceed to study behavior on the strength of these.

My own hopes for an approach to the new humanism which will give purpose, continuity, and even dignity, which to date it has not enjoyed, are most succinctly stated by Brewster Smith:[6] "We are at the threshold of ability to treat self-determination—free will, if you like—not as an illusion or paradox, not as a metaphysical assumption outside the grasp of science, but as an empirical variable that some persons rank higher on than others, a variable that is linked to causes and consequences that can be understood and turned to the enhancement of human freedom. A psychology that can deal with it empirically and systematically is both humanistic and scientific. I would like to help nudge psychology along in this direction."

The most difficult thing for anyone to accept is the untruth of that within which one has vested so much of one's integrity. It was like that with psychology and the question of morality. If psychologists were ever sure of anything, it was that the infant is born neither "good" nor "bad" from a moral standpoint, but that he learns his morals from his culture. It is now evident to the observing that moral principles, defined as behavior in relationships with others, is not totally relativistic to the culture into which one is born and within which one receives his teachings. Kohlberg[7] has opened this door with his careful research, and we can see that there are universal moral principles that are evidently programmed into the human genetic structure. How else could we explain how some of today's youth have moral principles which in terms of Kohlberg's stages range beyond any reinforcement (teaching) they could possibly have undergone. Of course, there will be strong resistance to such statements as these; and Kohlberg's research will be "laughed off" by many. Admittedly, it is only a point of beginning, albeit, an important one.

The dignity of man has been attacked; and that, in part, explains the progress we are making. When man is attacked, he will fight back. He fights back with whatever weaponry he may acquire. In discussing Kohlberg's research and Etzioni's proposals, Sampson[8] made an astute summary statement: "Darwin made man an animal; Freud gave man impulses that made him seem dangerous unless controlled; Rogers and Maslow made man good and potentially healthful and creative; the views of moral development we have been examining made man trustworthy in that the normal course of his development is toward generally beneficient principles of human justice."

The string of events among psychologists is now making sense. Psychology began as a science by splitting off from philosophy; in an attempt to gain scientific status, the discipline seized upon the format of behaviorism. The human being was written out of the equation. But man would not tolerate such depersonalization and psychology, during the '50s and '60s, became saturated with philosophical treatises concerning the human situation. The instinct theories were both overplayed and unmanageable from a scientific point of view. Armchair philosophy was unacceptable because it was obviously an exercise in foolish opinionativeness. But under scientific behaviorism man was losing his place as a dignified, intentional creature.

Mankind is presently reasserting his dignity. In the past quarter of a century he has fought against the oppressions of behaviorism with a revival of philosophies such as existentialism and the new humanism, which, while being somewhat out of phase with scientific psychology, have received widespread acclaim.

Psychology as a science shall need to search for a new identity. It will find such an identity in time; and when it does, mankind will be at front-center stage again as a special creature genetically endowed with the capacities of humanizing qualities such as love, kindness, the need to give and receive affection, and a morality that transcends the culture. While this is all happening (and it will take a long time), man will be receiving his clearest affirmations from philosophical sources. Whatever these sources may be, they must attest to man's human condition, countermanding the hurtful effects of behaviorism, denigrating religious legalism, dehumanizing technology, and culturally allowed reinforcements of violence, crime, and the devaluing of life.

In the interim—while scientific psychology regains its identity —man will continue to assert his human qualities of freedom, responsibility, and dignity. He must do this philosophically, for the most part, while he waits for the new psychology.

Chapter Four
Freedom: The Fountainhead of Dignity

The capability to make a choice, the freedom of will, is the fountainhead from which spring forth all the qualities of human life that ascend to create human meaningfulness; then, having reached the apex, form the luminous corona of the fountain of life—human dignity. Without the capacity for intentionality (free will), man could have no dignity except in the most limited sense; and even any form of dignity would be unlikely without freedom.

And so, if we speak of dignity, let us also speak of freedom. The one must be carefully considered before the other can even be plausible. Yet, freedom—especially as dealt with in the "freedom literature"—is a very complex concept, one that will at best always mean many things to many people.

Like happiness, freedom is many things to many people. When men are in chains, they see freedom as a release from

41

those chains; when under political oppression, they cry out for self-determination. When self-determination is achieved, even in relative measure, men point their thoughts of freedom to higher goals yet—to the freedom to "become persons," reacting with their worlds at their maximum potentials.

One would think that eventually the cry for freedom would be hushed. But that does not seem to be so. Never before has there been such an obsession with freedom. The more freedom man has the more he wants. Is this simply because man is by nature like a spoiled child always wanting more? Probably not.

MAN'S SEARCH FOR HIGH-ORDER FREEDOMS

More than likely, the louder, more persistent voices and the intellectual quests—resulting in many volumes written on the subject—come from mankind's sensing the possibility that a long-hoped-for goal may be coming within reach. As the realization of possible high-order freedom appears, man presses with even more zeal, compulsivity, and uneasiness than ever before. The uneasiness that accompanies such a search is undoubtedly a part of the human condition—it seems born of the realization that what seems possible may actually be snatched away at the last moment. All freedoms have been like that—they have been slow in coalescing either in philosophical common understandings or in substantive action of social reform. Being obsessed with lesser freedoms, man could not spare the energy to search out the deeper roots of his being. Hopefully, now he can begin to exert his energies toward what Maslow and others have termed "self-actualization," the action-oriented becoming.

Man's movement toward higher-order freedoms is most likely a function of having achieved some more pressing low-order need fulfillments. But beyond that, we are seeing a distinctively new phenomenon. In modern man we see a reactionary confrontation with several powerful philosophies of life which man has hated for a long time, and against which he has tended to rebel.

FREEDOM-ROBBING CONCEPTS

For generations now, man has been told that he is not free—that his acts and thoughts are derivatives of determiners from his past as well as his hereditary predispositions. He has been told, too, that he has no dignity. Various models have been proposed for human behavior, including the machine model and the animal model. Most such views are extremely pessimistic. In spite of these views, men who have given much time to intellectualizing about life and behavior—although their faith in themselves as intentional human beings has often wavered—have always really believed that man had freedom of choice and intrinsic worth. Ironcially, the unsophisticated have less difficulty avoiding the pitfalls of pessimistic philosophies. They simply feel that they *are* free, dignified, intentional beings; the religious heritages of many of them told them that they are, and they believe it implicity. Their more intellectual contemporaries have had to "sweat out" pessimistic philosophies which they found difficult to deny but despicable to accept.

It seems likely that most intellectuals really believed that they had freedom and dignity, that they could "will" their behavior in violent contradiction—if need be—to the determiners which unquestionably *did influence* their actions, or to the manipulators that imposed unwanted and unnecessary restraints. But the intellectual was forced to listen to pessimism, to cringe beneath pessimistic philosophies of the nature of man and his behavior. Man—even the most intelligent and intellectual—had inadequate tools with which to oppose determinism and manipulation while presenting a strong position in favor of the freedom and dignity he somehow knew he had.

Almost a century of constant exposure to Freudian psychology has contributed to man's feeling that his behavior is a function of his instinctual heredity, his past, and his present environments. True, the tenacious hold of this particular view, which condemned man to his instincts and previous experiences, is beginning to slip. Determinism is no longer the chief enemy of man's authentic freedom and dignity.

Among the relatively unsophisticated Westerners, there has always been a strong measure of what has often been called "rugged individualism." This philosophy of the American frontier was made up of strong reliance on oneself and an attendant belief that one could order his universe. Whereas determinism has undermined the belief in intentionality for one group (the intellectual), a creeping type of environmental control has swallowed up many others. Determinism has been tearing at us from within a theoretical framework, whereas the prevailing economic and political systems are destroying man's freedom and dignity in "fact" as contrasted to "theory."

The "organization man" is threatening to replace the rugged individual. Most workers of today do as the system dictates. And with industrialization, man has lost much of his freedom. Whyte[1] calls the organization man the person who not only works for the organization but one who "belongs to it as well. . . ." In this sense, man's freedom and dignity have been subjugated by the "system."

Indeed, the technological revolution under which man now struggles threatens his dignity in dozens of ways. All of these offshoots of technology converge to depersonalize the individual. Through technology, man often loses his employment, his sense of being, his status with his peers, his sense of privacy. The accumulation and storing of computerized information about his personal life and history, and his inability to act with discernment when faced with the enticement of modern advertising are only a few of the technological threats.

In his recent book, *Beyond Freedom and Dignity,* B. F. Skinner[2] has synthesized and crystallized from his lifelong views and numerous important works serious implications and threats to viable concepts of human freedom and dignity. The basic tenets of the Skinnerians have been reviewed in Chapter One. To have human beings controlled by elitist "human engineers" is understandably nauseating to most of us, who clearly believe in the "inner man" principle which Skinner so thoroughly denounces.

Perhaps the chief detractor of freedom and dignity for the individual is man himself. Mysteriously, man seems to be his own worst enemy. A creature of conflict, man appears to desire the best for himself and at the same time continuously wants to initiate the worst for himself. This duality of man's nature is contained in many views of man ranging from the original sin concept of the Judeo-Christian ethic to the life and death instincts suggested by Freud.

For many, the better life and the better world is contingent upon man enlarging his motivation to control selfish motives, to work not only for *his* own welfare but for the welfare of *his fellows*. The sustained failures of such calls made upon man's supposedly basic integrity make us wonder if such enticements to see, recognize, and act upon his viable choices, can ever really solve the problem. Clearly, man has not yet been able to activate the better side of his inner self so as to eradicate war, hate, poverty, bigotry and the like from his world. Can it be he simply does not understand? Does he need more education so that he will be informed as to the results of his actions? Can he be taught to successfully blot out his own selfishness, his own actions which doom him and his world to grosser quagmires of human defeat and misery? This we may hope. And for this reason, intellectual pursuits such as this writing may be justified, and may hopefully provide a part of the answer to the deep dilemmas of our torn world.

NEW PHILOSOPHIES ARE EMERGING

But things are changing. After so many years in which intelligent men were forced to concede by default to the deterministic view, now new and viable philosophies are emerging which are challenging the hateful, pessimistic views that made mankind a virtual prisoner of the past. It even seems probable that texts such as *Beyond Freedom and Dignity* will rouse rather than douse man's passion for freedom and dignity. Nothing motivates man to action like a vicious assault upon his personhood. On the other hand, it is possible that man may now be at a point where he can clearly see how the technological revolution with its foundation stone of materialistic valuing is defeating his own best interests.

Chief among these new emerging philosophies are existentialism and the new humanism. New trends of thought concerning the nature of man are calling individuals to an awareness of their existence in its essential freedom. Man not only becomes the greatest mystery of all, but the most important value in a confused and ambiguous world.

But are these philosophies really new? Did the ancient Greek philosophers not insist on man's freedom? Did the writers of the Holy Bible not declare over and over in favor of man's basic freedom?

Of course, they did. But somehow the powerful voices of pseudosciences have for centuries kept these teachings relegated to the status of folklore, biased and unbased revelation via divine inspiration. As such, they have largely been excluded from the thinking of "intelligent" men who have had a yen for the scientific.

So, thank God—or, if you prefer, thank fate or happenstance—for the reality of new, more optimistic views of man's nature and his clear-cut intentionality in all that he does and says. Man clearly is not a machine that can be reduced to an assortment of parts and systems. He is not an animal that has no capacity for standing apart and looking at himself. There is no model for man except man himself, as Sidney Jourard[3] affirms. Man transcends all things in this universe; thus, he will fit no model.

Say it as you may, man has freedom and dignity! And this assertion, which was never doubted by the devotees of conventional religion, can now be accepted by the most liberal intellectual. Support has been provided through carefully derived philosophies based not on experimental science but on observation and logic and, most of all, on experience. At last, the assertions of ancient religions are finding parallels with carefully derived logic from the minds of creditable and believable wise men of our generation. Although many experiences go beyond language, those who have these experiences have been able to communicate and to be understood by their fellows—not *in toto,* of course, but meaningfully nevertheless.

Perhaps it may be counted a shame that we have had to struggle so hard and long to come back to basic truths enunciated so many years ago by so many wise men of the past. A brighter view would permit us to believe that the wise men of today may expand upon the expressions of confidence in man's uniqueness and freedom from the past, give more concise interpretations of these, and bring us even closer to ultimacy in truths and freedoms. Men seem much more inclined today to take seriously experiences which would heretofore have been written off as mental aberrations. Although such experiences go beyond language, they do not go beyond credibility.

So the cry many men make for freedom and dignity is in reality a cry of exultation. *Man is free!* Oh, no—not free in the last analysis as touching upon each day-by-day contingency of living; our practical freedoms are limited and relative, and we do not now need to get sidetracked on that issue. For now, let us exult in the intellectually based, new-found concept of man's intentionality. Man has the capacity for freedom—not that he has already achieved perfect freedom, whatever that may be—and this freedom accentuates his intrinsic worth.

FREEDOM AND THE HUMAN CONDITION

With every obsession, with every exultation, comes the danger of overreacting. Perhaps this *is* happening in the context of man's freedom and dignity. With man's seeming rededication to his intentionality, to his transcendency over the determiners of his capability of seeing the dangers of technology and those other dangers which may be inside himself as a possible creature of weak nature, perhaps he should raise the questions, "Is perfect freedom a desirable thing? Or is it true that some restraint of freedom is desirable, even a security-producing action?"

Historically, freedom of political nature has been bought with many prices. Man's belief in his freedom of choice, especially in the face of so many contraindications of the validity of such choice, has undeniably placed him in many cruel quandaries. With belief in their freedom of choice tucked away in their hearts, thousands of people from many nations through many eras have sucked in their empty stomachs and made obeisances to rulers who oppressed them and capitalized on their need for bread in denying them their freedom—freedom at any and all levels.

Dostoyevsky,[4] in his *The Brothers Karamazov,* portrays Christ coming back to the world upon which he had placed the burden of freedom. He stands meekly before the Grand Inquisitor who says, "Thou wouldst go into the world, and art going with empty hands, with some promise of freedom, which men in their simplicity and their natural unruliness cannot even understand, which they fear and dread—*for nothing has ever been more insupportable for a man and a human society than freedom.* What is that freedom worth if obedience is bought with bread?" And still again in the same conversation, "No science will give them bread so long as they remain free. They will understand at least that freedom and bread enough for all are inconceivable together."

Man has suffered, is suffering for and from his freedom. It is a mixed blessing, but one from which man seemingly will not turn aside in his search. So, if man is denied his freedom at every turn, in the last analysis, from what and to what can he even hope to be free?

There is every reason to question whether or not freedom is possible or even desirable. It seems safe to say that it is possible—at least, relatively so. Man seems convinced more than ever before that since he has it, therefore it must be possible. Any reasonable person would know that his experience of freedom is in practical, everyday situations only a partial and fragmented thing.

It is well worth pointing out that the individual seldom experiences complete freedom pragmatically. With every initial choice he makes, he subjects himself to consequent choices that are required in order to actualize the initial choice. For instance, the young man who—with the most complete freedom one can conceive—chooses to be a surgeon, therewith renounces potential future freedoms which might have been enjoyed had he made another vocational choice. In studying for academic excellence, he must subject himself to freedom-robbing discipline if he wishes to realize his initial choice.

Ultimate or absolute freedom must be seen as something to be sought, not to be gained. Our active intentionality is, in one view, the result of the superior intellect that makes it possible for us to stand aside from ourselves and, looking to the future, analyze our present responses as to their effects upon our future events. Or, in the religious view, our freedom may be thought of as being brought about because of the entry of the Divine into our persons via a Holy Spirit which is able to give us freedom of choice through the indwelling.

Whichever way we choose to look at it, we will probably arrive at the conclusion that freedom is possible within the limitations imposed by our past histories, our present realities, and our beliefs in our future possibilities. And we will probably surmise that from whencesoever freedom might have come into the human situation, we can no more give it away than we can give away our very humanity. In a sense, we are stuck with it, like it or not.

THE PAST IS NOT THE FINAL ARBITER

We do not have to yield to the past, but we are inevitably influenced by it. We can rise up against the influences of our pasts, and we may succumb to these influences—they are often very demanding. But still, our evidence of freedom is not in *winning* the battle with the past but in our ability to *do* battle with our determiners.

We have a choice in every act. Sometimes the choice is to drift with the tidewaters of past experience. After all, most of our past directs us where we would wish to go in pursuit of happiness and security. Sometimes, in deference to our past experiences, we choose the "good" way—according to prevailing cultural standards—bringing us contentment; sometimes the past forces us—against our will—to choose the "bad" way, causing us unhappiness through conflict of various types and sources. One should logically ask, "Is it worth the price I would have to pay?"

Many have said, "You can be what you want to be." But we recognize the reasonableness of this has certain limits. These limits may be absolute, as in the case of a crippled boy wanting to break the school record in the hundred-yard dash; or they may be relative, as would be the case if a person of limited intelligence wanted to become a physician. But although we must retract some of the fervor with which we may first have embraced the idea of becoming whatever we want to become, this does not mean that we should accept defeat and decide that our fates are laid out for us—that we can do nothing about the matter.

Obviously, some of these influences of the past are what might be called unconscious motives; and, therefore, they render our decision-making much less than perfect. But we must still insist, in spite of all this, that in all of life's situations, men have a power of choice—to accept or to resist. They may be victimized by their pasts to some extent but, under certain conditions, they will be able to rise above them. Moreover, those who are at the total mercy of their pasts are likely to be the mentally ill, not the essentially normal persons.

BECOMING A REAL PERSON

What does it mean to become a real person? It means that we must build our lives out of the fabrics of realities and exercisable choices that are given us, choosing the better way, wherein choice is either possible or logical. And beyond that, it means accepting ourselves in those aspects wherein the fabric of our lives is imposed by heredity and by prior events, whether these have left their marks on our physical structures or on our personalities. Stated somewhat after the self-actualization principle voiced by Maslow and others, to become a real person means to exercise those choices we have toward becoming the type of persons we would like to be, and of coming to a comfortable knowledge and acceptance of ourselves as we are and of our self-possibilities.

It should be perfectly obvious, moreover, that individual performance in becoming a real person varies with age. For young children who are in the formative years personality-wise, it behooves parents, teachers, and others to insist on the building of a personality which, according to the best judgments and in relation to the culture in which the person may be expected to live, will prove to be the most wholesome and which may in all reasonableness result in a happy life for the growing youngster.

As one reaches the age of maturity, he must give his attention more to the matter of accepting and adjusting to the kind of person he has become during the formative years. At the early adult stage, the determination of what one should do about becoming a real person is more difficult, for the person is faced with the fact of his relative flexibility and his growing inflexibility. It is an age for deciding whether to work hard, make wise choices, and to change personality or to move toward truly becoming, in awareness, that which one has already become in fact. And, of course, an individual may decide on a combination of these two. His decision will in all likelihood be based on psychological economy—whichever can be accomplished with less cost and more reward.

So the challenge for young adults is to determine what choices they *can make* relating to an improvement in themselves as best they are able to evaluate. Beyond that, the challenge is to calculate the economy of change against the economy of coming to know and to be that person which has already evolved through heredity and experience. The person you are is most probably an acceptable person in terms of prevailing cultural standards—no one is perfect according to some cultural evaluative scheme of perfection, neither in body, intellect, nor in personality. But one can *know* himself, *like* himself for what he is, and *accept* his being as the most valuable asset he possesses. He can become more truly himself with positive self-regard—happy just to be himself.

The concept of becoming a real person has been succinctly expressed by Carl Rogers[5] who says, "It seems that gradually, painfully, the individual explores what is behind the masks he presents to the world, and even behind the masks with which he has been deceiving himself. Deeply and often vividly he experiences the various elements of himself which have been hidden within. Thus to an increasing degree he becomes himself—not a facade of conformity to others, nor a cynical denial of all feeling, nor a front of intellectual rationality, but a living, breathing, feeling, fluctuating process—in short, he becomes a person."

THE BASIC FREEDOM
IS THE FREEDOM TO BE FREE

The child who jerks away from a protecting (freedom denying) parent to run into the street gains his freedom at too great a cost. We may surmise the parent is correct in denying the child this type of freedom. Many adolescents and even adults have brought themselves hardship, shame, and suffering with heartache for their loved ones while foolishly demonstrating to the world how free they are or can be. Every exercise of freedom requires that we count the costs. What is man really seeking in the name of freedom? Is it not that he wants the freedom to be free? He may not choose the freedom available to him, because his judgment may dictate the foolishness of it. We lose our freedom entirely, and sometimes even our lives and social position when we exercise freedom in opposition to sound judgment.

One thing is certain—complete freedom is not desirable. Another thing is even more certain—an insightful recognition of man's ability to be freer than he is now would result in a much richer and fuller life for every man almost regardless of how one may define the terms *richer* and *fuller*.

MANKIND IN CONFLICT:
LIFE FORCES VERSUS DEATH FORCES

Scientists understandably do not accept the idea of self-evident truths. If any such "truth" could be defendable, it would be that there is an innate tendency of all organisms to value their lives. The adage "self-preservation is the first law of nature" is evidenced all around us in all forms and levels of life.

But there are exceptions to any truth. Suicides offer an exception to the norm of self-preservation. Obvious, long-term, self-destructive acts offer less dramatic exceptions. Such acts as overwork, overeating, or driving oneself to the brink might be properly seen as exceptions to the rule that every organism has a basic tendency and striving to protect his life from demise.

Few would argue this self-evident truth. A point of reality is offered, however, when we consider that man is, as Dostoyevsky says, constantly refusing to do all the things which are beneficial to himself. As Dostoyevsky[6] sees it, this capriciousness is a testimony to man's volitional condition. Man must prove to himself that he is free by volitionally foregoing the rule of self-preservation.

It is clear that man values life; and out of his "sense of life," as Ayn Rand[7] describes it, comes his tendencies to honor not only himself but others as well. Out of this sense of life comes self-love and love for others. Love is two-dimensional: man loves others as an attitude of appreciation or adulation, inasmuch as the other has enhanced his life. On the other hand, growing out of his sense of life, man acheives a capacity for a love *of* or a concern *for* the lives of others. Thus, man is capable of both "appreciation" love and "concern" love.

Is it possible for nurture to overcome nature? We do not know. If man succeeds in destroying himself and his planet, then the answer will be self-evident. But there will be no one left to ponder the answer—except in the sense that the persons who exist into these last days of the human race may come to answer this question affirmatively. Indeed, some fainthearted are saying even now that man's "bad" nature will overcome his life forces. And, I suppose, we all need to concede this possibility. It does seem that a trend is building toward the annihilation of mankind and the planet. Late studies by the President's Commission on Violence and by researchers such as Eron, Lefkowitz, Huesman, and Walder,[8] are showing that constant exposure to violence is bringing about a dramatic change in the human capacity to tolerate and engage in violent acts.

As we go into this last quarter of the twentieth century, we can see that our survival, to date, has been in part the result of the helpful though repressing effects of various organized religions. Man has survived because he has believed that his "bad" nature was condemned. So long as man lived in the ethical tradition of various "thou-shalt-nots," he was, through these repressive admonishings, able to control his "bad" nature. Man has been able to perpetuate society and keep murders, rapes, violences against persons, and self-destruction at levels so as to preserve the planet thus far, although the foundations are certainly shaking. The preservation of the planet has been possible, at least in part, because man has believed that he would be punished, not only through statutory law, but by being condemned to some type of punishment by forces outside himself and outside this world. Thus, repressive ethics and rules may have saved man for centuries; we cannot know what has been the total effect of these forces. Is it possible that man by nature being governed by life forces can suffer a reversal in such a manner that death forces will dominate? Realistically, it does seem possible, if not imminent.

We are living in an age in which death forces in man are running amok. The reasons for this are several: (1) the denouncement of "establishment" and codified religious values has removed repression from man's "bad" nature; (2) a large-scale overreaction to freedoms gained from the rejection of all primitive and repressive controls is flooding the world with acts against persons that seem to deny man's ability to love others while underscoring and exalting his self-love; (3) this self-love—which, in itself, can be a redeeming aspect of human behavior—

running amok in the masses, denigrates man's capacity to love others; and (4) people have become so apathetic under these duresses that they are unable to recognize and resist the dehumanizing forces which impinge from the technological revolution and from the ambitions of elitists, some of whom honestly believe that planned and total control of the human being is the only way out of these dilemmas.

What shall become of man now that the powers of thou-shalt-not ethics are slipping. If a man is set free from shackles of threatened punishment—whether immediately enforceable by man-made law, or enforceable through making him apprehensive about receiving "justices" for disobedience through the wrath of whatever god—then where shall he find the "enforcers" designed to regress his "bad" nature thereby keeping his "good" nature in control? Having been set free from repressive threats of punishment, man is now vulnerable to self-annihilation. Basically, he doesn't know how to control himself now that he is out from under these threats. With the waning of repressive ethics, man finds himself in a peculiar dilemma. There are only two answers: either man will become obsolete in an eruption of violence and self-mutilation, or some means must be found to restore the predominance of his inherent "goodness."

It is clear that without repressive ethics man shall have to go back to a reassertion of his life force. Which way shall it be? Shall it be a control of the masses by wise and hopefully benevolent elitists, or shall it be a return to a belief in personhood, human dignity, and man's capacity to control himself through his own inherent life forces. There is absolutely no doubt in my mind that there is one and only one way. We must reassert our dignity as human beings vested with life forces that, in some mysterious way, place men at the apex of creation. These life forces can save man—and nothing else can! Man is much more good than bad at this point in history. He must become succinctly aware of this; and he must come to know that a reembracing of his own nature for good is his *only possible salvation!* He must not allow himself to be led down the road to control by elitists. Such control would further destroy man's eroding life forces to the point where he could never recover his dignity or his destiny.

Chapter Five
Moving Toward
Self-Esteem

It may be reasonably argued that dignity or self-esteem is not a condition. Rather, it is a feeling. It is like being rich or being poor. One man may envy his neighbor because the neighbor owns a secondhand automobile. This neighbor may feel himself to be the poorest of the poor, stymied by and hating his poverty. It's like that with freedom and dignity; the feeling is what counts. Without self-esteem, the individual can never be even minimally happy or well-adjusted.

This is not difficult to accept. But what about the person who to the casual observer is bound by the most stringent bonds? A wife with six children is in virtual bondage, never getting away from the oppression of the household. But she doesn't realize, doesn't feel her bondage. Is she free because she does not *feel* bound? And does she suddenly feel unfree when she reads certain women's liberation literature? Let us, for the sake of discussion, suggest that the answer to both questions is yes.

According to the concept of phenomenology, reality for any person is what *he* perceives. If he feels free, or doesn't feel unfree, then reality for him is freedom and dignity with high levels of self-esteem. By the same token, a person who, judged objectively, has a large measure of freedom but who feels totally restrained, feels no freedom; therefore he experiences no freedom, no dignity, no self-esteem.

AWARENESS OF LOSS OF FREEDOM

No person who really dwells on the subject can believe himself to be totally free. Every human relationship is bought with the price of relinquished freedom. Perhaps Thoreau was freer than most, but we may wonder if he was free from the oppression of boredom. No person who thinks intelligently on the subject wants to be completely free to the exclusion of all human relationships. It's too insecure, too dangerous. We need these human relationships, although binding, very much. Yet every person who gives thought to it is likely to find himself straining at his bonds, wanting to feel freer—to be freer than he feels he is.

Whatever else we may say about freedom, no man wishes to admit that he isn't free. Indeed, there are many who will adamantly claim they are "free as the breeze." But when pinned down to reality—or made aware of their reality—they realize they are bound—not free at all. Many assert their freedom as a defense against an unwanted awareness that they are not really free at all. It is a very questionable act of "friendship" to make a person aware of the factors that block his freedom, factors of which he was happily unaware before he was told. Such an act is certain to undermine self-esteem.

This is often the case in psychotherapy. The therapist thinks that one of the greatest services he can render is to point out the areas of life in which the patient is bound. If these bondages can be broken, reasons the therapist, then the patient will be set free to grow. Well and good, if we posit ultimate value in the growth process. Manifestly, many are better left in the status quo where they are functioning very well, feeling free enough with a modicum of happiness. It does little good to tell a mother of six how bound she is when, as a matter of fact, she feels pretty good about her "enslavement"—an enslavement seen by the observer, but not felt by her. She may possibly be made aware of her loss of freedom and then feel that she has lost something very precious. Left alone, she may not have felt particularly free but, on the other hand, she may not have felt unfree either.

Over the years, the American people working through the United States governmental functionaries and agencies have invested billions of dollars and thousands of lives on the proposition that oppressed peoples should become unoppressed; that is, unoppressed within the purview of what has been euphemized as "the democratic ideal" or "self-determination" translated into group political actions.

Few persons are ready and willing to condemn all such purported acts of humanitarianism. In some cases, these philosophies and actions have been brought into the service of liberating people who knew that they were oppressed. In other cases, the American ideal of freedom has been urged and implemented upon persons who did not feel unfree.

It now appears obvious that great tragedy has come because of impulsive acts of government—acts which tended toward the American ideal of freedom without bringing into question either other ideals of freedom or the question of felt freedom as opposed to seen freedom. As a nation, we shall probably continue some intrusions into the lives and politics of other nations while suffering for many years from previous incursions into the not always viable concept of "setting the world free from oppression." As a nation, we must learn lessons from the past. Such lessons, learned at optimum levels, may not deter us from other intrusions; but at least we *can be aware* of the possible implications of our actions.

LOSS OF SELF-ESTEEM WITHOUT AWARENESS

It is one thing to be unaware of bondage, thus being allowed a subjective feeling of relative freedom and contentment. Sadly, it is yet another to feel a loss of freedom and self-esteem, actually to respond to this loss with mental and/or physical illness, but to be unaware of what is really wrong. This is the picture we often get of the neurotic or psychotic who is ill from oppression, yet has not been able to identify his illness as a loss of freedom or of self-esteem. He couldn't verbalize his difficulty, yet he feels unable to cope with his world.

Sometimes it is proper to speak of the person experiencing this type of loss as being the victim of unconscious forces operating in his life. At one level on the conscious-unconscious continuum, a woman could suffer a breakdown which had its origins in the boredom of an automated, suburban household where she has not even the companionship of her husband. The husband is supplying her with all the comforts of modern life—an automobile, color television, and expensive clothing—and she has the fulfillment of children, yet she is drying up inside from boredom.

There are certainly cases where the counselor, minister, psychiatrist, or neighbor, comes to the conclusion that a person must be made aware of the cruel bondages that are making him ill. This focuses upon the judgment required of helpers as to whether or not the best wisdom lies in forcing persons to accept their loss of self-esteem, to feel it, and to cope with the results of it toward the regaining of lost health. It is a soul-searching question for any counselor who is able to realize and to analyze the possible results of his intrusion.

All of this brings us sharply back to the realization that every individual is a law unto himself. It is grossly unfair to make people unhappy by pointing out how their sense of self has been objectively lost when, as a matter of fact, they are not feeling this loss. It is just as grossly negligent to allow a person to wallow in a quagmire of mental illness, or even deep frustration, from which he may never escape unless someone points out to him that his condition is related to the loss he is unaware of but which is surely a cause of his distress.

Sidney Jourard[1] suggests that mental illness is "a form of protest against a way of life that is not fit for the person who has been living it." He further deplores the actions of doctors and psychiatrists who do a "patch job" on the individual, fixing him up with drugs and supports that make it possible for the patient to return to his "hell on earth" simply to become ill again when the supports do not work anymore. He becomes ill because of the nature of the life he is living; and to Jourard it makes better sense to change the life than to give the patient treatment that will enable him to bear the same horrible nightmare, usually only for a limited time, until he has to return to the physician for some more veneer to encase himself in. It is like building a life-support system for the patient, and permitting him to stay on the moon rather than removing him from the moon where he could not live without support.

It is easy to give credence to this idea. Perhaps men should be removed from their moons (situations which will not support life, wherein they will only wither and die). Unfortunately, the problem cannot be so easily resolved. Removal is not always easy—sometimes it is impossible. However, it is easy to concede that more effort should be lent to correcting hateful life situations and less to providing a tenuous support system for staying in such a despicable world.

For every case of mental illness, there is logically an expediency. For some who are older, have bad hearts, etc., the expediency may be to hold them within the framework of the life that makes them ill simply by helping them adjust to that life. For the young and virile, it may be suggested that a continued searching for a way of life in which they can live without becoming repeatedly ill is expedient.

But then, it would be a great mistake to suggest that all mental illness is a revolt against an unbearable life style. Much mental illness is a direct result of bad situations in the past and present for which the person is improperly conditioned. Excising the past influences of a trauma may make living in the same life space perfectly safe and rewarding.

Just as the barnacles must be cleaned from the hull of a ship in order to "free" it for a better journey through the water, man must fight battles with influences from his past. There is little commendation for fighting the battle without help when help is available.

THREATS TO PERSONAL FREEDOMS

It is possible for one to lose large measures of freedom without being aware that he is losing anything at all. Thus he would not *feel* his loss. The truth is that there are a great many robbers of our freedom even in a society that seems so free. Our society has spawned many "pickpockets" that are robbing us of freedom while we feel no freedom loss at all. In the name of a growing political and economic freedom, we are being managed; and we are expected to smile and allow these "benevolent despots" to take control. And these forces are gaining.

Advertising is a pertinent case in point. We are being poisoned by drugs and pleasure-products while swallowing a bunch of lies to the effect that these products are giving us a long-awaited freedom. We pay more for a small package of rice just because it is packaged a little differently than another packaged with one-third more rice. Merchandising and salesmanship are manipulating us. The manipulators are learning their how-to's to the tune of books with names like *How To Manage People* and *How To Break Down Sales Resistance*. In all this, humans are being treated like gullible robots.

A truth-in-lending bill has been legislated to make it possible for us to see how much we are being robbed through excessive interest rates.

But the manipulators are winning out; our lives are no longer our own. We are being caught up in a system that propagates itself through clever and subtle controls. We buy things the manipulators want us to buy whether we need them or not. The paradoxical aspect is that most people have a firm conviction that they are real pros when it comes to sales resistance. So, again, the loss of freedom is there in an objectively defined reality while the claims are quite to the contrary—in the name of freedom we are being duped into losing it.

How long shall we continue to be lulled to sleep by our visions of freedom while the world closes in around us, chuckling as we become more and more the robots of such a vampire system? Is such a system necessarily a part of a way of life which brings us higher and higher standards of living? Maybe the cop-outs are the only ones who can see the creeping enslavement of materialism. For most of us, the anesthesia is so pleasant that we do not mind parting with our excised vitals, while, behind the facade of freedom lurks the spectre of a carefully considered system of control and human management.

Can it be that man's lack of freedom has less to do with his power of intentionality than it does with his ability to see his enemies? He cannot lash out to gain his freedom because he cannot see what he should be fighting. And the real enemy against man's freedom is not the diabolical past with all its so-called determiners so much as it is the present with its insidious human controls.

FREEDOM AND DRUG ADDICTION

Drugs are paradoxical agents. They can produce freedom—no doubt about it. When one has a headache, aspirin can make him freer. At other points, we shall discuss the liberating effects of the psychedelic drugs. But many drugs are great deceivers, and it is in this context that we now approach the topic. The point is that some drugs create feelings of freedom and euphoria while weaving a web of enslavement around the users. For the most part, these are the addictive drugs.

One side of the debate offered in this chapter is that as one feels, so is he—at least as it applies to freedom, dignity, and self-esteem. And perhaps this is true even in the case of feelings under the influence of drugs. Yet, in service to a broader truth (the ideal), we must recognize that temporary feelings are not always desirable, especially when there is a resultant loss over the long haul. Besides that, we have never been able to say that freedom—whether felt to be or objectively judged to be—is always beneficial. Neither should we assert with conviction that all freedom, or feelings thereof, brought about by drug usage is bad. It is bad only if the end result is a loss through dependence upon the drug. Even then, the good and the bad may be relative.

The release of inhibitions brought on by alcohol is, in itself, neither good nor bad. It might be good if it provided release from nervous tension; it might be bad if it resulted in so much freedom that the imbiber tripped over a rug and had a bad fall because he was experiencing so much release.

We may be tempted to generalize that a feeling of freedom brought about by a drug is a false feeling. Even so, the good may supersede the bad; but, in any system of valuing, this idea must lead us into the consideration of one's impact on others around him.

FOR ONESELF OR FOR THE WHOLE

Maintaining self-esteem is not synonymous with, but certainly is related to, what Tillich[2] was fond of describing as being for oneself. High self-esteem usually implies a type of self-centeredness.

The more mature person, however, is able to expand his concept of freedom—freedom in its fullest ramifications to include what Tillich[3] also has called being for the whole. Within this context, one's freedom should never transgress the rights of others. The socialized human can hardly feel happy when he realizes his behavior is hurtful or obnoxious to his fellows. Any defendable ideal always involves others as well as oneself. What is self-esteem worth, in the long run, if human values are abrogated in the process of achieving it? One man's freedom can indeed constitute another man's bondage as when the husband exercises his freedom to play golf at the expense of the wife who loses her freedom, bound as she is by household duties which might have been made lighter by a more helpful, loving, and understanding husband.

FREEDOM, RESPONSIBILITY, AND GUILT

The relationship between freedom and responsibility is obvious. If a person claims freedom of will, then he cannot logically disclaim responsibilities for his choices. Freedom puts the individual in the driver's seat. Errors of judgment and of action must be credited to the man who espouses freedom for himself.

Herein possibly lies the reason why psychoanalytical principles have been attractive to man, especially Western man. Having been reared under the concept of rugged individualism, self-determination, and responsible behavior, psychoanalysis offered man a bargain: give up your freedom, and the responsibility for your judgments and actions will be removed. As Marvin Frankel[4] has said, "Actually patients in psychotherapy, and particularly in traditional psychoanalysis, may be said to be trading precisely in this kind of currency—often purchasing a form of security at the expense of freedom." That Western man is reviling psychoanalytical principles is obvious; and this is a clear indication that he is almost ready to say, "Give me back my sense of freedom, and I will gladly shoulder the responsibility." How, indeed, can man ever *feel* free if he is not willing to take responsibility for the outcomes of his freedom? Even so, during the transition period there will be many who, not thinking these implications through, will try to "have their cake and eat it too." They will want freedom without responsibility. The claim may be well supported that this is exactly what is happening among rebellious youth today. Not that they do not have good reason to rebel; they somehow have not made the obvious connection between freedom and responsibility.

Guilt is a natural result of freedom and responsibility. Unavoidably, the person who feels free and who assumes responsibility will suffer from error and failure, especially if in the commission of error and failure he violates his values. So we shall have to face guilt if we are to have a sense of freedom.

The person who does not make errors is the person who ventures nothing; and the person who ventures nothing is not activating his freedom—nor is he implementing his responsibility. Our world is too full of needs—needs for the individual and for his fellows to allow him to go "scot free," making neither choice nor error, accepting neither blame nor guilt. And it is all too obvious that in our mushrooming world of critical, complex, and ambiguous situations, more and more judgments must be made, therewith bringing more and more calls for responsible action. And even with the exercise of the best possible caution consonant with the need for judgment and action, the probability for error rises. Thus, modern man must be ready to do something about his guilt feelings.

O. Hobart Mowrer[5] has been the leading evangelist for a new therapy, Integrity Therapy, which clearly recognizes the relationships between freedom, responsibility, and guilt. Mowrer feels that nothing is gained in trying to dissuade the neurotic from feeling guilty over transgression of his own values. Since man has "sinned" in the sense that he has violated his own values, then he must pay the price for his guilt. A "confession" is needed in order to restore the person back to a redemptive community fellowship where his "sins" may be forgiven and the person may once again feel accepted.

This format for therapy holds promise as an implementation for the handling of the type of guilt feelings which may be felt most clearly by the person as alienation from his fellows. Obviously, in a more strictly God-oriented view, the person may need to make his peace with the transcendent God or, at least, to the god whom he conceives and deifies.

It should be more than obvious that guilt must somehow be handled in the psychological economy of the person. Unless guilt is handled, the person not being able to receive absolution from his "priest"—the psychotherapist—through assurance that he was not free to begin with, is not responsible, anyway. Therefore, he need feel no guilt, and will simply renounce his freedom, withdrawing from the world of responsible action. He will do anything to escape the burden of guilt since it is much easier to give up freedom, deny responsibility, and thus escape guilt.

But this is the pattern of neuroticism—a progressively more restricted world in which the individual feels more and more "lost" and stripped of meaning. It is clearly a losing game and will ultimately rob us of our most cherished human quality, a clear-cut intentionality, a true feeling of worth. No, we shall not settle for a more constricted life space and world view. We *must* find a way to handle our guilt and continue to maintain self-esteem.

In service to a more inclusive truth, perhaps we should be reminded that guilt is not the inevitable result of responsible judgment gone awry. There are great individual differences here. Some persons are more capable than others of taking their failures in stride with a philosophical "you can't win 'em all" attitude. In other words, failure brings self-blame in relative strength to various persons differentially.

Nor is it true that unresolved guilt is the only force that can drive a person into a neurotic trend, a restricted life space where he has many fears and will not venture forth into the broader world even on an experimental basis. The evidence is replete that guilt will do this; but it is just as conclusive that hurtful experiences of childhood can ramify into a neurotic pattern— experiences wherein guilt is not the most obvious factor, if a factor at all.

Even so, freedom-robbing neurotic trends do develop from unresolved guilt. In the Freudian view, the demon involved is an overly strict superego, the result of harsh training in values at the hands of legalistic parents—values which when abrogated usually do bring guilt. Values so strictly laid down are restrictive in themselves on the one hand, and "set the person up" for guilt and loss of freedom on the other.

Many intelligent persons have escaped the webs of their superegos, recognizing the constricting effects of harsh values. Some have been able to replace these "learned" values with a new set, and are living relatively free but responsible lives. But this has seldom been easy with or without psychotherapeutic help.

Such values as these are usually introjected from parents and "swallowed down" without basis in the experience of the individual. Rogers[6] describes these values as "introjected or taken over from others, but perceived in distorted fashion, as if they had been experienced directly." Such values may be described as "unconscious"; thus, are powerful restricters of a viable freedom.

Chapter Six
The Existential Posture and Human Worth

Neither the intellectual community nor the nonintellectual community can be clearly defined. It is true that there is a growing intellectualism, and the hillbilly image is fast disappearing except on the television screens.

There *is* a roughly defined community wherein the process of thinking out problems, of writing books, of reading and discussing philosophical ideas are principal interests. If we still had to fight Indians and dig stumps from the new ground, we should have neither time nor inclination to be intellectual. But we are all about through digging stumps.

A large number of people, especially among the college-age youth and recent graduates, are philosophizing more and more; and new ideas are emerging. Many of the so-called new ideas are simply old ideas in new cloaks but they are being expressed in more viable forms.

FREEDOM, ELITISM, AND
CONTROL—ON BALANCE

It is true that the proponents of freedom, self-will, equality, and justice-for-all have been guilty of hanging their philosophies on a star while allowing their practices to be aligned just short of the gutter. Thus the viability of a future of man oriented to freedom and therewith denying the need for human control has been weakened.

Democracy as practiced in the United States, for instance, far from ever being an exercise in perfect self-determination by a majority of either a franchised electorate or the population at large, has been a rule by a vocal and power-based minority. True, it might well be argued that this is the way it has had to be and must continue to be, that the ignorant and uninformed, for their own good, must be protected by the elite. The trouble is, as we all know, that the power-based minority has been too often guilty of promoting their own self-interests either individually or as a reference group of high status seekers rather than the interests of the entire citizenry. Thus, the poor will be with us always and various social ills seem destined to perpetuate into eternity—or at least until the planet is destroyed.

It would be comforting to the freedom advocates if we could only declare with emphasis and with justification that the right will eventually triumph if only we make clear the case for freedom of the will and allow man to seek his own ultimate best interests—man's yen for his own advantages would ultimately get him to a near, if not a perfect, utopia. In this, however, we are forced to reckon with a reality that suggests that man does not always pursue what to any reasonable man would appear to be his best advantages. Indeed, as Dostoyevsky[1] —himself an advocate of freedom—suggests, man's most advantageous advantage is that he may exercise his caprice and choose to do things which work toward his disadvantage, even his extinction, with a clear knowledge of what he is doing to himself.

Whether placed within the context of man's capriciousness—his seeming determination to do the unexpected (in

70

terms of his own advantages), perhaps in order to avoid the stultifying ennui; the horrifying boredom of having to do all the right things at all the right times—or within the context of man's selfishness (achieving his own good without concern for others), we arrive at the reality that man has not to this date made a very good world.

There is good reason for men to entertain the question of whether man may indeed be in a better position to save the planet by yielding his capriciousness and his selfishness to some elite controllers. This, of course, is the basic idea behind Skinner's *Beyond Freedom and Dignity*.[2] And, in giving credit where due, it does seem now that Skinner's concept of a controlled environment, as voiced in 1971, is a control vested in a larger and more cosmopolitan group of controllers than seemed to be suggested by the much heavier-handed controllers of *Walden Two* developed by Skinner in 1948. Thus, Skinner's new formula for control seems more like the elitism of the so-called democratic society where, in reality, men are controlled by a myriad of forces largely outside the scope of consciousness, foolishly thinking all the while that they are free.

There is disturbing evidence that man, in the last quarter of this century, will fail to change the direction of destroying himself and his planet if left to the status quo of controls in the name of self-determination, or a false democracy. Witness the economic situation of the 1970s in which controls had to be dictated by the federal government in order to avoid economic disaster. The evidence is clear that the people could not muster the self-control necessary to halt inflation and economic catastrophe. Is this necessary surrender to controls on the economic front not a sufficient analogy to show us that man cannot voluntarily turn a tide seemingly set in motion by his own basic selfishness and by his capriciousness?

It would be easy to say yes. Man has always been controlled, is now being controlled toward a disastrous end, and must (according to the Skinnerians) be recontrolled toward a trend and direction, decided by high-level elitists to culminate in a better chance for his evolving a livable world, saving the planet, and redeeming man to a much less dangerous community with his fellows.

One segment of the intellectual community is saying yes to this need for control. But even as is true in the economic analogy, others in the intellectual community are saying no. It may even be that some are at the point of saying yes now (as in the case of economic controls), but maintain the high hope that we may stay man's headlong plunge toward a crash into oblivion by a type and level of control while giving him reeducation on the principles of freedom eventuating in the hopeful removal of controls and a voluntary and sensible understanding of the price that must be paid for freedom. Perhaps man has too long believed that freedom is free. *It is not.*

FREEDOM AND THE EXISTENTIAL POSITION

The intellectual community is definitely taken with a group of expressions coming from the writings of persons who, for one reason or another, choose to call themselves—or are called by their followers—existentialists. The designation is by no means a clear-cut one. But the term seems to be here to stay, and patterns of meaning for the term are in process of jelling.

As difficult as it is either to define or describe the existentialist position, there are at least three things that stand out as common denominators. First, there is a firm and unyielding insistence on man's freedom. Man is an intentional creature who can cast off the yoke of his determiners and, at a point of time and space, can exercise his free will. That this position is almost identical to the religiously based position of freedom-of-will is not always recognized. This clearly constitutes the resurrection of old principles that have become obscured, rather than the birth of totally new ideas.

Perhaps the real difference is that the traditional religiously oriented people have always claimed to posit man's intentionality as a gift from God, while the philosophical existentialists claim that free will is purely a product of man's humanity. It seems necessary to suggest here, however, that the existentialists are of two rather well-delineated groups with one continuing to posit "essence" or an innate value and meaning in man, while the other claims man only has "existence," which is to say that whatever meaning evolves *for* man must be produced *by* man. Sartre,[3] in setting forth these groups, used the terms *Christian* and *atheistic*, and included Jaspers and Marcel among the Christians—himself and Heidegger among the atheists. Sartre's term *Christian* is unfortunate inasmuch as this group obviously should not be so narrowly described. This dichotomy has well been expressed in other writings as the Wedding versus the Divorce (atheistic) Existentialists.

The second strong common denominator of existentialists is man's responsibility. Freedom without an attendant responsibility is unthinkable, perhaps for the very practical reason that such freedom without responsibility would surely result in chaos and obliteration of the human race.

The third common denominator is a firm belief in each man's uniqueness and dignity. From the existentialist viewpoint, man is clearly a creature set apart. He is a person, not a thing; and man's responsibility extends outward toward others to give them the dignified status of being treated like *persons* and not used as *things*.

Existentialism is definitely a rebellion against some despised ideas and practices. The philosophy clearly breaks with determinism, dictatorship in whatever form, statism, prejudice, oppression, and poverty—especially that produced by man's inhumanity to man.

Existentialism clearly moves out from the key position on man's freedom, but its full expression obviously curbs exploitative freedoms, those utilized by one man at another man's expense. It is again a rebellion against present forms of politics, philosophy, and even religion. The chief criticism leveled at existentialism is that it seeks to destroy present forms without taking the responsibility (so clearly enunciated for the individual but not recognized as applying to the group who call themselves existentialists) of proposing and enacting reforms necessary to make their philosophies operant. But this is understandable, since the existentialist idea proposes that the *individual* is responsible. The individual must be set free to be responsible without coercion that comes from position-taking by another individual or group.

THE NONINTELLECTUAL AND FREEDOM

There are those who take great pride in pointing out that many of the dignitaries who lived in Old Testament times were existentialists. There are those who say that Jesus Christ was the forerunner of existentialism; some ascribe to Socrates strong existentialist leanings. Even so, it is to Kierkegaard that the title of Father of Existentialism has most often been given; and we suspect that this title has been given posthumously for the most part.

Who is, was, or was not, an existentialist may bring us confusion. Revelling in the title is not the all-important thing. It is unavoidable that certain positions regarding man's freedom, responsibility, and dignity have, from the time of recorded history, been clearly expressed and strongly implemented in human action.

It is unavoidable that the teachings of Socrates and Christ laid a firm foundation for the same type of existential thought and action being championed today. It is clear also that the lives of many persons are the epitome of the now-recognized and symbolized existential position without their ever having heard the word *existentialism*. The unavoidably sad report must be made that there are millions of people, most of whom would be called nonintellectual by almost any agreed-upon definition, who mouth their convictions of existential propositions in whatever name—sometimes in the name of Christianity, humanism, Jewry, etc.—who belie their stated convictions by the grossest violations of these positions.

Can we charge all of the hatred so extant in the actions of self-styled religionists off to lack of insight? Perhaps this is the only way we can respond if we ourselves are to have human compassion and recognize the dignity of man, even among those who seem to act in ways we cannot condone. But beyond that, can we not at least hope to make them aware of what they are doing?

We must remember that every one of us is subject to this human frailty, to violate unknowingly or unwillingly the very tenets we espouse. It is easy for us to spot the person who uses the man of the minority group as a thing to be exploited for his personal gain economically. We can be blinded to our own actions and motives which violate the same ethic at a different level of human relationship. The most adamant crusader for civil rights may be ignoring the personal good of his own wife and children because he is so intent on lambasting the devils who use and abuse the minority groups. Violations of the existential positions can be blatant or they can be subtle. Moreover, what is seen as blatant to one person is not seen so to another. Intellectuals are blind to their own violations while seeing clearly the cruel hypocrisies of those they identify as the bourgeoisie. As Salvador de Madariaga[4] puts it in his classic *Portrait of a Man Standing,* "This is perhaps one of the most paradoxical constants of modern intellectual life; prejudice even in those who think themselves the freest of the free."

FREEDOM AND THE WORLD AROUND US

The Divorce Existentialists accept all the basic concepts of man's intentionality. They are adamant in saying that man is not only free, but that man *is* freedom. Man has freedom to make choices, to move against the grain of his determiners. And it may be said that these persons are fanatic in their insistence on man's dignity and responsibility. But the distinguishing feature for these philosophers is that they view the world around them as totally hostile. They are sure that nature or the nonhuman world ultimately will triumph over them. Nature will eventually bring them to the grave, and thus, will have the ultimate victory. Man's freedom is to move against the forces of a hostile nature, to rise up in righteous indignation to the relentless, damnable pressures of the world. Man can spit in the eye of nature and maintain his human dignity right up to the point of death. This is the basic position of men like Sartre and Camus. There is, in this view of freedom, a forlornness that seems very sad to the Wedding Existentialists.

The Wedding Existentialists see man having the same elements of freedom, dignity, and responsibility. Yet, they believe that somewhere in the background there is some indefinable force—although it is clearly defined for certain subgroups in various ways—which says that life is not hopeless, that man *can* triumph over nature. These, especially the Christians, would say with Christ, "O death, where is thy sting? Oh grave, where is thy victory?" Certainly all the Wedding Existentialists are not Christians, but for each subgroup there is redemption for man, there is a reason behind it all. As Hallie[5] says, "They are the reconciled ones, who find in nature ciphers, traces, hints that men may read and thereby learn the ultimate meaning of it all. Behind the blank, brutal face of nature they feel a redemptive force to which we can hopefully give ourselves."

Sartre[6] says, "All human activities are equivalent . . . all are on principle doomed to failure." The Divorce Existentialists see the Christian, the humanist, the religiously oriented persons as escapists who are creating gods to escape the brutality of a nature which is hostile. They see the hopeful ones as cowards who will not face facts. For them, a greater freedom lies in man's acceptance that there is no hope—for if a man has hope, he becomes subservient to a system of values that undergirds that hope, and he becomes enslaved not only by the false hope but by the system that offers support to the hope. If a man is a Christian, he is bound to the tenets of the faith and to behavioral requirements that he sin not.

Strangely, while the Divorce Existentialists do not wish to lose a part of their freedom in subservience to a system which involves a set of thou-shalts and thou-shalt-nots, they appear as committed as any group to the dignity of man and to his welfare. Paradox of paradoxes, we sometimes are forced to concede that there are stronger evidences of human concern in the actions of the Divorce Existentialists than in the Wedding Existentialists.

It goes without saying that the rank and file of non-intellectuals do not classify themselves either way, because they are unaware of the terms, let alone the distinctions. But the two groups live among us nevertheless. Logic might suggest that the people without hope of a redemptive force would themselves become ruthlessly exploitative, grabbing every pleasure for the moment. From this group would thus come the criminal element. To a certain extent, this is true. But our judgment and observation, if not statistics which may one day be available, make us aware of the fact that criminal acts proceed from the ones who claim to see a redemptive force in nature—at least as much in proportion as from those who see the world as a hopeless quagmire of human frustration.

Our ground is not firm here, but we cannot but be amazed at the indicators pointing toward the possible fact that members of our beat generation—most of whom would be in the Divorce camp—show indications of great capacities of love and compassion. Witness the groups of radical youth who, even though indulging in seeming acts of carnality, demonstrate a knowledge of love far beyond that of their rigid, legalistic, supposedly mature parents. Is it possible that the so-called rebel demonstrators are at heart convinced of the inevitable victory of nature over them and yet are able to embrace the concepts of man's dignity, worthwhileness, and his need for love? Such evidence as we have and the writings of the Divorce Existentialists add substance to this seeming paradox that the capacity for love somehow exudes from every human personality. Those who believe in man's freedom, dignity, and responsibility in the context of forlornness, the certitude of inevitable defeat, and the nothingness of death, also know about love. For these, man has dignity even in the face of certain and inevitable defeat, and that dignity dictates a love relationship among human beings.

THE THIRD FORCE IN PSYCHOLOGY

Behavioral science has made tremendous strides in the direction of understanding, predicting, and controlling human behavior. Indeed, it is more than probable, as Oppenheimer[7] suggests, that there will be much more sober, grave, and emotional response of the public to the possibilities of human control growing out of behavioral sciences than that attached to the abilities of natural sciences to control matter and to conquer space.

The impending capacities and realities of behavioral control as a scientific endeavor, together with the subtle controls already with us—derived from persons and institutions which selfishly design projects (such as in advertising) to control us—is probably responsible for the emergence of what has been described as a third force in psychology.

Psychology has long claimed distinction as a behavioral science, constantly perfecting its tools and methodologies for answering questions about behavior. Learning much about the antecedents of behavior has made the control of behavior come easily in reach. Psychology has engaged in the helping professions of counseling and psychotherapy together with behavior-modification procedures directed toward clients and patients who may be expected to benefit from these ministrations. That these helping professions constitute a type of control may be quickly conceded. Psychoanalysis and behaviorism in turn have flourished and receded in importance. These two forces in psychology are being superseded by a third; namely, a new philosophical dimension most often referred to as humanistic psychology, the aim of which is to reassert the freedom and the dignity of man within his power of self-willing. The proponents of this third force in psychology are many; and, at least in America, the new humanism and the human potential movement is strong and growing. Moreover, anticipation is strong that an empirical discipline will be based on this new humanism.

The new humanism can be compared to existentialism, which has always had more of a European origin and which has, to say the least, been vested with certain mystical qualities that removed these doctrines of the nature of man from any reasonable scientific approach either for determining its validity or its outcomes. Thus, the new humanism has a greater plausibility, if not a richer heritage, than existentialism for many American psychologists and other behavioral scientists.

While humanism and existentialism have much in common, the former is much less philosophical and far more subject to enlargement by scientific inquiry than the latter. The new humanism, the third force in American psychology, asserts itself against the call of the behaviorists and Skinnerians for a calculated control of man. That man can be controlled is not the question; that man is being controlled is not the question. That man must be forced to yield to calculated control in order to save himself and his planet is the issue; that he *may be* forced to accept control for survival is conceded with great reluctance. The humanists are fighting for the dignity of man, believing that his dignity will be lost if he *must be* forced into controls, thereby losing the essence of his humanity.

In short, the humanists are not willing to concede on the need for calculated controls. They are more convinced that behavioral science can and should be used to accentuate man's freedom rather than to engineer his control. In presenting their case for freedom as the most cherished concept in man's survival, the new humanists deny that the only way out of the dilemmas into which humans have fallen is human and environmental control. They believe that objectively determined control is impossible, for every control mechanism must be the result of a value which predated the control effort and lies outside the control mechanism. They believe that any effort to control must first confront these questions: Who will control? What type of control will be used? Who will be controlled? Why is control necessary? Humanists will never be convinced that controls may be managed without an elitism, for values and sophistication, as well as power, must emerge somewhere within the paradigm. Humanists are hoping desperately to be able to rekindle the desire for autonomy; they do not believe that calculated controls must come just because subtle controls are already occurring.

It is obvious that humanists believe that man's freedom is of such a nature that scientific knowledge of man's behavior is possible. They believe that behavioral science may be brought to the service of making man more pragmatically free rather than of dictating his control.

It is obvious that there are other positions beyond those of the humanists, positions which suggest that man's freedom removes him from being a fit subject for scientific inquiry. In general, these forces reside in persons whose systems of beliefs posit a supernatural, divine, or spiritual force that, being outside of man (while perhaps also being within him), are able to direct man in such ways as to make human behavior unlawful in the last analysis; that is, man may be subject to influences that both deny and obviate the purported laws of cause-and-effect.

MANKIND AND NATURAL MORALITY

There is a distinct drifting away on the part of the young from organized religion. With this there seems to be a heightened sense of social consciousness. Both Sartre and Camus have expressed beliefs that in spite of the forlornness of the human situation we are all responsible for each other; and this philosophy certainly brings a possibility of love to the most rebellious.

There are many possible explanations for the phenomena we are now observing. Obviously, it could be explained that the seemingly natural morality that comes not because of organized religion and often in spite of its sometimes shortsighted philosophies and projects may be due to the intrusion of a divine force of love in the lives of even those who are quick to disclaim any supernatural source of their morality. If this is not the case, then we may at least suggest that there is an inborn humaneness in humans—a humaneness that is often obscured and negated by the forces of hypocrisy extant in a competitive and materialistic society. And these elements obviously infiltrate organized religion.

On the other hand, we should not be naive concerning the evidences of love among the hippies and other groups that espouse love. All does not meet the eye. One has to venture only a little way down Haight Street to become aware that in the name of love, carnality and exploitation of the grossest sort is rampant. It is probably true that some of the original hippies espoused a type of love that was indeed redemptive while being disassociated with both organized religion and materialistic society. There is good evidence that these people have tried to escape the madding crowds of the curious as well as the hordes of joiners who came not to be a part of the new love, or even of the new morality, but to delight in the sensuousness of the situation. Many have been attracted to the hippie colonies not out of motives of humaneness, social reform, or social isolationism, but because of the presence of a multitude of morally loose pleasure seekers. Because of this, in part, the drug problem has risen; and under the guise of the flower-children image a truly barbaric society has evolved which has turned a reasonable new morality into a crass replay of old immorality themes and actions.

The question of a natural morality is not yet answered. There are good evidences of a solid morality (dedication to a non-exploitative human relationship) outside of organized religion and the controlled materialistic society. Where are the origins? It cannot be assured in the present that they are natural origins, innately posited in the human person and condition. There are too many thousands of responsibility-abandoning and pleasure-seeking youth among the few purists to make it possible for us to make an accurate judgment.

Chapter Seven

Transcendental Behavior

Transcendency is a strongly evolving concept in American psychology and, more generally, in American thinking. European existentialism has invaded American thought, rescuing us from the traps imposed by psychoanalysis and other ideologies that left the individual hanging by his unconscious. True, Americans borrowed these pessimistic philosophies from the Europeans, so perhaps it is a type of justice that we should be delivered by another European philosophy.

Values now are being posited back in the individual instead of in some psychic or cosmic force outside or in political, religious, and economic theories. Nietzche may have contributed to this with his "God is dead" philosophy. And the god who existed in men's minds only outside of themselves is *dead*. Man has been forced to turn his thoughts upon himself as the source of values. This could mean a return to basic humanism or it could herald an approach of a new Christianity or at least a new God-centered religion or system of thought. If the Great God of the Universe out there is dead, it may mean a revivification of the Great Indwelling God. This, of course, *is* the position of religious existentialists.

No matter how you look at it, the focusing white light is being turned upon the individual. The human animal is no longer being seen reductionistically, as a machine, that can be taken apart and the parts counted as so many components of a system. No longer is the whole equal to the sum of its parts. Rather, the functioning whole is greater than all of its parts.

Can man actually experience transcendental behavior? First, we must consider the meaning of the term—only then will we be able with intelligence to approach the question of man's capacities in transcendence. Transcendency means the human capacity, through his intentionality, to order his universe in opposition, if need be, to the dictation of the possible determiners of his behavior. Beyond that, transcendency (as in Kant's philosophy) means experiencing beyond the limits of organismic (human) possibilities, thus transcending our natural experiential sensors and receptors.

TRANSCENDENCE AS OPPOSITION TO DETERMINERS

We have already proposed that man can willfully do battle with his determiners. Our only proof is that man is doing it. He *feels* he is doing it. It may be man thinks he has freedom to deal with his determiners out of his intentionality, but is a victim of self-deception. Possibly so. But let us be content with the rules of phenomenology. If man thinks he can go against his determiners, if he feels this freedom, he actually has it.

A principal goal of psychology is to predict man's behavior. Can man's behavior be predicted? Our position is that man's behavior could be predicted if (1) we knew what all his determiners were, (2) if we were able correctly to know what effect these determiners in summation or in multiplication would have on behavior, and (3) if we could know whether or not man had renounced or resigned his will to go against his determiners. Given that man has been so subdued that he really believes that he had no power of the will, then he would obviously renounce such will and it in return would become noneffective. Given that, we might be able to develop skills for prediction if we knew what the determiners were, their relative strengths, and their directions. Even so, this would be a difficult task. It is an impossible task unless we know, at least for the interim, that man has chosen not to violate his determiners. And even then we should be most skeptical, because we could not know at what moment man might change his mind and pit his intentionality against the determiners.

There is no doubt that man functions typically in a reduced state, that he most often follows the dictation of his culture, that he conforms to what is expected of him. When he occasionally does the very unexpected (shows our predictions to be wrong), when he does rise to great heights of experience, becomes truly creative, etc., we could simply say that there was something about his determiners that we did not understand before.

That is always the possible out for the determinists. Actually, it is practically impossible to convince the skeptic who does not believe in man's capability to transcend (do battle with his determiners). The out is so simple. If man rises up and violates his determiners, this rising up was simply another determiner unknown until it was expressed. Perhaps a hereditary aspect, which has somehow defied analysis, has crept in to ruin the prediction.

As often as not, the creative genius is labeled mentally ill and is ostracized. Most of us simply play it safe and conform. This brings about three possible conditions: (1) we become estranged from much of our possible experience because we know in advance that it will be socially disallowed, (2) we repress our experience of freedom, or (3) we renounce our freedom of experience. This renunciation really does reduce us to types of robots who, having the capacity for transcendence, slip back into the comfortable niche of conformity. If this continues to happen, we will someday actually be victims of our determiners. We will be like the pigeon who after two hundred pecks and a sore bill never pecks again. It is a wonder that this hasn't already happened; indeed, it has happened to many of us. We are beaten down never to peck again. Happily, many of us are more like the pigeon who pecks and pecks, and being rewarded at least intermittently, continues to pursue goals, because it believes that finally it shall be rewarded.

THE ANXIETY OF MEANINGLESSNESS

Rollo May[1] has described the human dilemma as man's being able to experience himself as subject and object at the same time. Both are necessary. Man cannot live in this objective world without thinking of himself as an object that must be manipulated even by oneself. Each of us is manipulated by our needs to make a living and to get something done so that we will receive recognition. As May[2] says, we are "objects of time," and manipulated by it.

As a subject, "time is open before me to use as I choose." My contention here is that I am subject not object, and I have freedom to choose. As much as I might like, I cannot always be subject—I must yield to being the object acted upon much if not most of the time. Our competitive world is made that way.

Our capacity to will ourselves into the subjective mode produces a strain, or an excitement. So long as we are in the objective mode of existence, being manipulated by time and socially produced need fulfillment, we are in the process of losing our significance, our meaning. It is not entirely so, of course, for we may have a type of significance involved in doing our jobs well, etc. It is clear, however, that our deeper experience of significance is in the subjective mode when we feel that we "are in charge of our worlds." Total acceptance of the objective mode leaves us feeling depersonalized.

Depersonalization is definitely a loss of freedom as well as a loss of meaning. The human being desires recognition of others and the personhood of self-approval above all else. The great social upheavals we are now facing may well stem from the feelings of depersonalization. The rebels likely are reacting so that they may be noticed, and this may be as important to them as are the causes they espouse. The faceless student known only as a number on an IBM card has become the standard of meaninglessness against which not only the student but his adult counterpart constantly fights. Many writers have given assent to this type of anxiety. This type of anxiety proceeds out of a lack of meaning and of purpose in life.

Although few would phrase their dilemmas this way, it is a question deeply embedded in the life situation of each of us. How can I escape the objective mode and move into the subjective mode? Can I somehow transcend my determiners that force me to lose sight of myself as a person and agree to become a thing? Surely this quandary is at the base of current obsession with transcendental behavior. In seeking a way out of May's dilemma, too many of us are not content with the happy middle ground of being object when we must and being subject when we can. We are hungry for the experience of meaning, and we seek means of expressing our transcendency. Our compulsivity of effort as often as not becomes the bucking horse that throws us off and turns around to trample us.

TRANSCENDENTAL BEHAVIOR AND MEDITATION

Most of our lives we are responding to the world in terms of our needs. We are looking ahead toward the delectable dinner we hope to have. We view the sunset with the intent to soak in the beauty of it; we read a book for relaxation. In this sense, we are never free from ourselves—from our transient needs and states.

What would happen if you and I should lay aside every human need and concern, either by completely ignoring them or because all needs were satisfied? What would happen if we should just let go and let be? We should be terribly bored, of course, since we are not accustomed to such a state.

But what we have been describing is roughly what does happen to the Eastern mystic as he meditates. Some call it transcendental meditation. This is also roughly the state of the hypnotized person. He is responding to his being, not to his requirements. And, under such conditions, the mystic or the hypnotized person experiences quite a different world, since it is uncolored by his need to make pretenses for his fellows' sake or to satisfy his own needs. Things just happen. He is in a state of being himself. It sounds quite entrancing, doesn't it? We may be certain that this produces states of rest far beyond what most of us experience in the quiescent state we call sleep. We may be sure that it is an act that can be achieved only with much concentration and practice. We seldom see transcendental meditation in the Western world for we move too many projects outside ourselves to permit it. On the other hand, most of us would be inclined to think a person would have to be a little touched in the head to try it. We may even resist the temptation to try it, for we fear it is a state from which we might never be able to return. There is a similarity between transcendental meditation and certain forms of schizophrenia.

Such a state of letting-be involves something more—at least, most of the time it does. In the case of the hypnotized person, it requires a complete trust in the hypnotist, a capacity to take his suggestions without fear. Similar states of nirvana or satori in the terms of the Eastern mystic can be brought about only if a person will sit at the feet of his guru, who, seizing upon this perfect trust of his subject, guides him into a state of transcendental meditation.

We are reminded at once that this state of complete trust and relaxation is achieved by many in the Western world in their lives of prayer and meditation within the contexts of their religious experiences. Here the complete trust is in God, however he may be conceived. But as J.B. Phillips[3] has expressed it, "Our God is too small," and most of us cannot muster this degree of trust nor this degree of relaxation under the "shelter of His wing." Most religious persons seem to have lost this capacity. "Come unto me all ye that labor and are heavy laden and I will give you rest," falls upon deaf ears, for most people do not have the ability to separate themselves from their worlds of self-need and self-fulfillments sufficiently and have not the trust sufficient for this journey. Such a separation is indeed frightening. It must be something like sky diving, just letting go and letting be, trusting one's parachute.

THE PEAK EXPERIENCE

Maslow,[4] in his book *Toward a Psychology of Being,* speaks of the experiences in life reported to him by many that seemed to transcend their previous selves in moments of life's greatest ecstacies. Maslow refers to these experiences as "peak experiences" or as B-cognitions (*B* abbreviating *Being*). He offers, by contrast, the D-cognition (*D* abbreviating *Deficiency*). Maslow gives us more insight into the peak experiences by describing them: "B-love experience, the parental experience, the mystic, the aesthetic perception, the creative moment, the therapeutic or intellectual insight, the orgasmic experience, certain forms of athletic fulfillment, etc. These and other moments of highest happiness and fulfillment I shall call peak experiences."

Maslow's treatment of such peak experiences does not claim transcendence in the sense that the human being goes out beyond his capacities for perception, thus peak experiences are not metaphysical or ultrahuman. But they do have a quality not found in the typical deficiency (need-oriented) experience which makes up most experiences of Western man. Among other descriptive qualities of the peak experience are: (1) detached from relations, usefulness, expediency or purpose; (2) irrelevant to human concerns; (3) ego-transcending; (4) carrying its own intrinsic value; (5) disoriented in time and space; and (6) only and always good and desirable.

All of these descriptions suggest that whatever else they may be, peak experiences are free from needs and pressures to conform. They represent transcendental freedom from the usual workaday world. Properly understood, these experiences speak to the uniqueness of man who seeks release from his controls. They have a sublimity which suggests that they are matters of choice for the individual pointed in a direction away from an environment that would try to control.

Dostoyevsky,[5] in an especially cogent observation on human nature wrote, "Out of ingratitude man will play you a dirty trick, just to prove that men are still men and not the keys of a piano." Men can manipulate other men up to a point, but beyond that point man will rebel and he will lay aside all controls; he will transcend his sometimes cruel, sometimes dull and sordid world. He will create for himself experiences in which he may revel.

Man's seeming need for worship experience may fall in this vein. "Religion is the opiate of the people," said Karl Marx. Yes, it is that, without doubt. Maybe it is much more.

GOING BEYOND ONESELF

The peak experience and the letting-go-and-letting-be are both well within the inclusive concepts of humanism. These are experiences a free man makes for himself but only within the range of his possible behavior. This is perhaps human behavior at its possible human best.

The bigger question yet concerning man and his possibility of transcendency is in his capacity to go beyond his own organism—even beyond the capacities of his physical organism to experience thrills and pleasures, or pains and sorrows.

The exultations of the holy men from many religious groups are rich in suggestion that transcendence may move beyond the human condition and the perceptual and experiental possibilities of the human organism. The psychedelic drugs are seen by many users as capable of transporting them beyond themselves. The Eastern mystics seemingly feel they achieve similar goals.

At once we find ourselves in the throes of a vexing debate. Can the organism have experiences that are not within the organism's capacity? Are not such so-called metaphysical experiences possible only through an extension of the *usual* perceptual capacities of the human body?

It is a sterile debate. It gets us nowhere. There are many who claim experiences beyond what Maslow calls peak experiences.

With easy assurance, the spiritualist, the drug user, and the mystic may say that they receive extra receptors with which to receive these experiences. They may say it in the sense that they are organismically equipped with hidden antennae which are extended only in time of such transcendental experience, or they may posit that these extrasensory receptors are granted to them within the context of a spirit world. One may claim with impunity that he has a separate-and-apart spiritual self with which to experience these transcendencies. Or he may say that an indwelling spirit lends him extra equipment through which he receives on spiritual wave lengths.

It is true that most research in ESP is in disrepute, but it would behoove us not to pass judgment on all of these claims. We no more have the power or the logic with which to disclaim them than the proponents of ESP have to confirm them.

To the strict determinists, humanistic psychology is just as indefensible as ESP. Man is controlled lawfully, and that is all that there is to it. To most determinists the humanists have opened the door to spiritualism. It is difficult to deny that the direction away from determinism is the same for humanism and theism. Theism is only a little further down the same road. It is just a little more transcendental in nature.

Chapter Eight
Human Life: A Showcase of Dignity

Here we are, humans all, caught up in the webs of a complex and confusing life situation. We each shall live for a certain number of days or years. None of us will ever know just how long he shall be alive. That death is inevitable can be viewed optimistically as the beginning of a new and better phase of existence or as total nonbeing and nothingness as suggested by Sartre.[1] Moreover, some of us will be alive, continue to live physically, long after our mental facilities have ceased or greatly declined.

We are captives of a life for which we did not ask, which some may not even want. "To be or not to be" is not at all the question—certainly not the total question. We *are* and we shall continue *to be* for some time, captured by life.

True, we *are* in the sense that we are alive. But, on the other hand, we are not completely *alive* to all the realities that could *really happen* in us and through us. Beyond being alive, there lies the enthralling prospect of *becoming* (a forward movement) and of *being* in the sense of living each moment in time and space to the fullest of our evolving potentials. This seems to be the basic human urge, to move forward (become) and in the process of moving, to live optimally.

Humans will never be content just to *be;* that is, just to be alive. They must search for meaning in this universe, and make an effort to grasp the prize of a total encounter with life. No one knows what that encounter is like; most of us only know we have not yet achieved it. But history reveals over and over again the indomitable courage to be that has made man a restless adventurer in quest of all that life may *possibly* offer. This is another human dilemma. Man cannot rest until he knows all there is to know about life. And, of course, he never shall; thus man is committed to this restless adventure, always driven to becoming and being at higher and higher levels.

Man has now set foot on the moon and he *will* explore the planets. Why? Because they are there! Similarly, we will explore our beings—again, because we are here. We know we live and breathe, but we do not fully know yet in whom (or in what) we have our beings. We shall probably never fully know, but we shall always be seeking and finding. We shall have the courage to be because we have the freedom to search.

CAPTURED BY OUR CULTURE

We are captives of our culture—not altogether unhappily so, perhaps. But being children of a given culture with all the holds (or strangleholds) it has on us, does affect our freedoms, our new and sometimes radical ideas, our values we try so hard to express in a typically hostile climate, and the new projects we would like to try. Being alive places us in a capsule; culture shapes the capsule. And we have to break out!

Our culture would not be totally undesirable if it were a function of the principles of the present and foreseeable future. Inevitably, each generation is taught how to live in the culture which was shaped from the values of its forebears. In this fast-changing world, some cultural values and projects are outdated before a child comes of age. Yet he is held largely a prisoner within the capsule fashioned by his mentors. Obviously, this is not totally bad; in fact, change based totally on immature judgments would result in chaos. Yet, change must come, if human dignity is to be restored.

PUSHING AGAINST THE
WALLS OF OUR CAPSULES

In the life space that surrounds each of us, we are all, in a sense, trying to expand our freedom of experience—we are pushing against the restraints that hold us in the capsule. It may be that all of humanity is searching for the same thing. One could call it happiness, security, or equanimity. We are searching for a few hours of peace and contentment; yet somehow, if we really think about it, we surely know that such equanimity as we may be able to achieve will be relative—it will be happiness at some degree along the scale from a knowledgeable relief from pain and a quiet acceptance of the inevitability of life to the sublime ecstasy of the highest moment of awareness. This high point will be expressed and experienced by some as communion with a supreme being; for some, in the exultation of sexual orgasm filled with meaning in terms of man's highest creative act; and for still others, this highest point may come with a mind-expanding drug experience.

How can we best express the yearning in the human being? What is the base factor behind the highest form of experience, happiness, or security? Do we dare generalize what constitutes the base source, the matrix of human happiness, realizing that each of us is unique?

Many have dared suggest the basics of human existence and human yearning. Some have used the concept of meaning, others freedom, self-actualization, as well as religious concepts of salvation, of true awakening, and eternal life. These are common modes of expression, and they seem to have more commonalty than difference. It is worth considering that the expressions of Sartre, Tillich, Kierkegaard, Rogers, Suzuki and Christ were quite similar in basic meaning while being expressed in varying ways.

Man's possibilities of happiness are possibly threatened because he has become too knowledgeable—so knowledgeable, in fact, that he can no longer accept explanations just because someone (even someone in authority) has made these explanations, even though the acceptance of these explanations may have brought him a measure of peace.

Some of the self-styled intellectuals look with disdain at their bourgeois fellows who seemingly have leveled off too low in their search for meaning. They have leveled off in various ways, chief among which is the acceptance of closed systems of religiously based meaning. "Christ is the answer," or "Commit yourself to the church and find eternal meaning," are typical summaries of such closed systems of meaning.

For those who are judged to be not so intellectual by the self-styled intellectuals, the end of their search has been reached. Not perhaps that the end they have accepted *is* the inevitable end, but that they *believe* it is the unquestioned endplace of the search. These can supposedly go in peace with their security, their explanation of the *why* of their existences and the *wheres* of their destinies fully assured for them. Whether or not the answers they have accepted ultimately are the right ones is beside the question, *since peace is largely in believing that one has it.*

There is a sense in which the person who has accepted a solution to his human condition is the most fortunate of all. It simply must be so! If one really does accept the proposed explanation without further question, and if that explanation continues to hold for him through the days and years that he goes on living, it serves well. For, after all, what better way is there to evaluate a life than to say that for X numbers of days and years the individual thought he had a secure hold on truth and that he had attendant peace?

And so it has been. Many have lived out their years in such a state. Happiness and security have been theirs to own and cherish even though life itself may have been brutal. Who would want to take away from anyone this capacity to accept an explanation for existence and with it a way for eternal existence? Only the most cold, calculating sadist!

So, perhaps many of the books we have should never have been written, for these books undoubtedly have taken away the walls of protection furnished by a successfully operating capsule within which many human beings have lived out their lives and within which many still are living. And I confess that authoring this book is a chary experience I undertake with considerable trepidation.

The big question we must ask is this: Are all or even most humans *really* happy within their capsules embracing their concepts of reality? Are they successfully dealing with life's vexing problems behind their walls, or are they merely cringing there, afraid to look or question, fearing their security may be destroyed?

How wonderful to be able to live out one's life in the security of a system—a system that is never threatened within the total life space of the individual, from the time of accepting the system to the time of physical death. We could wish such a state for every human being who lives today! But inevitably those who are, with great security, hiding beneath the rock, are becoming fewer and fewer, and the number of cringers has far outnumbered them. Our world, with its mass media of communication, with its expanding knowledge, and with its yen for educating the masses, is bringing an end to such possibilities. Even more sadly, the vast numbers of the younger generation are neither hiders nor cringers but have broken with the faith and are afloat on a no-longer-tranquil sea. Manifestly, our world is made up now, in the main, of people with no anchors, with no walls behind which to hide or to cringe. In Frankl's term, they are in the midst of an "existential vacuum."[2] Meaning is gone with the ruptured walls of the capsule.

What can we who may be concerned do? Can we create new walls, or can we repair the old ones? We seem to have a number of choices; indeed these choices are now being implemented by the various professions—psychologists, physicians, ministers, etc. One choice is to bolster the sagging faith of the hider. There is little doubt that this is being done by many professionals who actually believe in the elements of faith that the hiders adopted. These are not confined certainly to the ministerial group, but it seems to me that a large number of such people are found within the religious context.

Hundreds of thousands of young people are taking their quandaries to their religious leaders and are receiving out of honest hearts a bolstering of a faith to which they no longer can subscribe. We would be foolish to pass judgment that this is wrong, because we cannot be sure that the elements of faith are anything but ultimate.

Our resentment should be reserved for the pseudo-professionals who are propping up sagging faith, a faith in which they themselves have no confidence. These are charlatans, and they are open to observation wherever one wishes to look. They continue to play upon the insecurities of those who have fallen through the cracks in their capsules. They reaffirm and exploit, not out of a basis of honest valuing of the faith, but out of their desires for the venerations of their followers. Such charismatic leaders are becoming wealthy as they receive the donations along with the adulations of their flocks. They exist on every continent and within every type of framework of faith— religious, political, and otherwise.

It is perhaps not right to pass judgment on such supposed exploitation, for we must confess that it is fraud only if the perpetuator really does not embrace the faith any longer. We may venture a guess that the majority of such people not only have personal qualities of charisma, but that they did at one time honestly embrace the tenets of faith.

THE HELPER FACES MANY QUANDARIES

Many are ministering to human need, honestly asking the question, "What is the best approach to use with this person at this time?" Trying to gain an honest answer to this question, many professionals are unwilling to break down what remains of the capsule even when they themselves no longer support the elements of faith that once made the capsule secure. What is to be gained by pressuring the disturbed person to abandon all shreds of his former world view—unless, of course, the professional has one with which to replace that which is abandoned? Is this a commendable duplicity? Perhaps it is. But often the professional who refuses to destroy a faith, knowing he has nothing with which to replace it, really feels he is being dishonest. His dilemma is a serious one. He can be consoled, however, in the belief that the true professional knows he does not have *an answer* to replace the emptiness that comes from giving up a world view or a faith.

Strangely, the gaining of professional status in the helping arts usually brings a loss of certainty concerning any system of values. The professional must place the welfare of his client uppermost in his own priority of values—and this invariably forces him away from authoritative stances concerning values.

Many professional persons are called on to make speeches, give sermons, etc., in order to help the people they address. Others are writing books for the same reason. The people addressed in speeches and writings represent many positions within the broad scope of tenets of faith concerning life. Can the professional express what he knows or even what he believes with strong assurance? If he does, he may in effect be stripping the walls from the systems of many persons. It is at best a terrible dilemma. It is reasonable to expect that a professional resolves this dilemma one of three ways: he expresses himself blandly on topics with little or no depth; he tries to assess the common denominator of tenets of faith in his audiences, directing his words to the majority as he has assessed them; or he moves forward on his convictions of the rightness of his position, accepting the possibility of hurting some people in the present in order to make life meaningful in present and future for many others.

If the professional adopts the middle position, it is not actually necessary for him to say what he does not believe; but he almost invariably will avoid revealing all that he is thinking, all of his own searchings and half-clear insights. It would be much too dangerous, not only to himself—perhaps least of all to himself—but to many in his audiences who would be pushed out of the comfort of their private capsules by an assault upon their fortresses. This is probably why there is less exhortative preaching from pulpits. This is why the open-ended search has become the standard vehicle for inquiry and exposition. Obviously, a proponent of the last position above should be a person of great courage and strong conviction. It is unavoidable that he *may* be a neurotic, seeking to obtain a measure of vengeance from a little-suspecting group of people.

THE OPEN-ENDED SEARCH

Is it not true, after all, that the only closing point with life is an open-ended search for what it (life) is all about? And is it not true that the open-ended stance protects one against the coercions of neurotics?

There was a time, perhaps, when there were no neurotics who, for reasons involved in their own private worlds, constantly endeavored to coerce others to join with them in their own special brand of hell on earth. If we accept the proposition that there was indeed a time when there were no neurotics, then we must suggest therewith that there were at that time no confusing and ambiguous circumstances of life driving individuals into conflict. Meaning in life was guaranteed on the basis of social systems that permitted no room for interpretation of meanings. Life was lived in unity of purpose for every person. Life might have been brutal in a sense, but it was never ambiguous—man scratched the ground to provide food crops, he fended off the enemy, he sustained himself in community, one that was unified and clearly understood as contrasted to our own culture. As we have it now, life's goals are ambiguous, its conflicts are constant, and those who have become neurotic are trying to get others to become as they are.

It is easy to believe that in primitive societies, judgments of good and evil were so integral to the social fabric that there was little questioning of the standards of conduct, hence little rebellion, loss of meaning, or overreacting (neurosis). Such a world obviously would provide a type of moral security which the people of the Western world, to say the least, do not have today. In the main, the values of today have become multidimensional, have become differentiated into systems called religion, science, and politics, among others. The medieval synthesis came about after the fall of Rome with the resulting denial of a unity in life and an assertion of the dominance of theology over science and politics. Thus the separation of the sacred from the secular evolved. This separation still exists for most persons.

It is true, however, that recent years have brought about a secularization of society. The medieval synthesis is no longer viable to the intellectual person. The post-Christian era is here, although lip service is still being paid to so-called Christian principles. For many, at least, this is done for cultural reasons, rather than as a consecration of personal faith. The Secular City, as per Harvey Cox,[3] is fast becoming reality, and the results are less than totally gratifying. This is usually the case during times of great social revolution. The situation is confusing for all of us, and most of us shift into the open-ended search to preserve sanity while searching for reasonably continuous realities.

Suppose we do commit ourselves to the idea that life is a never-ending search for meaning, a search for the source of our beings, for a purposeful fulfillment for being here at all. Should we conclude that an ephemeral happiness or peace is present within all who have adopted the open-ended stance?

No, this is not likely the case. For happiness is only partly in the search itself. True, there is a certain level of contentment that comes from knowing that everyone is searching, but that no one has found the answers. There is security in knowing that one is among a *community* of seekers. But contentment varies.

Some individuals are at points of believing that they are closer than some others to the end of the search. Again, it is true that feeling is the principal thing involved in the achievement of meaning. Positive feeling comes to the open-ended searcher who feels either that he is nearing the goal or that he is making progress. One person may feel excited over gaining a specific insight while another who has had many forward-looking insights may have now gone for months or even years with no new insights.

Even if we concede the need for the open-ended quest, we must still attend to the concept of the capsule in which we live. Even with the open-ended search, the ruptured capsule that spills us forth from itself too quickly is overpoweringly frightening.

No, we dare not explore too far outside the capsules of our culture, our past experiences, our introjected values. It is like the moon traveler who must not get too far from the module that will hopefully return him to the mother ship. We see our safety in the *familiar* past—in being a manipulandum. We are afraid (and justly so) to leave the capsule, and to the extent that we are afraid, our freedom is blunted, our human dignity becomes blighted. It is probable that our reluctance to leave the capsule is based on three things: (1) we cannot believe that our old way of life is completely useless to us, (2) we cannot see clearly what the new would be like, and (3) we are afraid of change.

Even though we observe the safety factor in the old capsule, we know that we may expand our freedom and dignity only through expanding our perspectives. "Where there is no vision. . . ." Unavoidably we have been too busy making a living inside the capsule to make a life outside it.

Chapter Nine

The Search For Dignity Through Personal Meaning and Identity

Aristotle said, "Not life, but the good life is to be valued." A few centuries later, Christ said, "I have come that you might have life and have it more abundantly." The good life is a relative thing, of course, but most of us would venture that we do not have it as good as we might hope. Thus, a search is in order, if we aspire toward the good life.

B.F. Skinner[1] presents a rather pathetic picture of the person in search of dignity via the positive reinforcement of praise and approval. "Praise and approval are generally reinforcing . . ." he says. "The amount of credit a person receives is related in a curious way to the visibility of the causes of his behavior."

In dealing with human dignity, Skinner insists that dignity is an assigned value, an extrinsic worth as contrasted to the dignity of intrinsic worth espoused in this book. And we must admit that Skinner's concept of dignity is largely acceded to in our culture. Indeed, the extrinsic nature of human dignity as espoused in our culture has affected all of us. The need for approval is one of the most powerful of our socialized needs.

We search constantly for social approval; many of our actions are tinged with an almost neurotic need for this acceptance. We must engage ourselves in constant search for this type of dignity. It constantly eludes us. We could logically be free from this need to search, but it is deeply engrained in us. And it is fortunate that man has the freedom to search for dignity, however defined. Only in the freedom to search can we finally come to know the freedom from searching. It is an interesting dilemma, and so much a part of being human.

How may we enhance the freedom to engage in that search? The zest for searching belongs to the relatively young, especially to college-aged youth. It is easy to see that many of the middle-aged and the old are seeking comfort not in the search, but in freedom from it. They are willing, for the most part, to rest upon the laurels they have. Whatever big insight they might possibly gain from searching further would come too late to justify the pain of the search.

But with the young it is or should be different. They search for the good life they hope they may have, and they have the zeal so necessary for carrying the search forward. Except in unusual cases, great leaps forward are initiated by the young, for the old are devoted more to whatever creature comforts the status quo might deliver. The youth is the conscience of every age, seeing as they do that the adults in their eagerness to maintain status quo in comfort have become hypocritically inconsistent in defense of the systems in which they have elected to live out their lives.

THE PECULIAR DILEMMAS OF THE COLLEGE STUDENT

Ironically, the relatively old seem busy throwing up roadblocks to squelch the search initiated by the relatively young. Professors and administrators play the data game with students. The student is pressured into an accumulation of facts that inevitably increase in such a stultifying geometric progression that he is always behind and getting "behinder" all the time. To use May's illustrations, the student is getting hit on the head by so many "academic apples"[2] that he is too groggy to know what is going on. He is fast developing into little more than an animated "fact bag."

Thus, the student loses his perspective. He loses the meaning of his original search. His values which, at first were his own, now have become geared to requirements that lay outside himself, that are indigenous to the educational enterprise. He is so engrossed with making scores on tests based on his acquisition of external knowledge that his consciousness is shrunk, and his experience of himself (his freedom to be) is undermined. He has become a pawn in the pursuit of purposes and projects not chosen by himself, but which are brought to bear upon him by his superiors. These superiors range from the inanely senile to the alert and sometimes radically inclined professors of the new left. But even if he is subjected to the sharpest and most level-headed avant-garde thinking of the best professors, he is still a manipulandum at the hands of his superiors. There are exceptions, of course—exceptional teachers and exceptional students—teachers who will not subjugate young minds, students who take the trodden chaff of the academic machine and kick it aside while the professor is not looking.

Typically, however, the student is subjected to anxiety and depersonalization. And although we may agree with Kierkegaard that "anxiety is our best teacher," we are inclined to modify this statement. Some anxiety does raise the students' level of need for new experience and sharpens their powers of acquisition. Other anxiety, depending upon its nature and severity as well as upon the recipient of it, blocks the freedom to search. The wrong anxiety will make the student neurotic, causing him to withdraw from the possible wealth of stimulation because he finds he must defend himself from within a narrowed world view or go to pieces.

Among the most refreshing innovations in this last part of the twentieth century is the trend toward a deschooling of society.

Many of us thought it would never come, so impatiently had we waited. But the employment trends of the early '70s which found Ph.D.s ready to take jobs in service stations have finally turned our heads in a saner direction. Emphasis is now being placed upon technical vocational training in a myriad of institutes that, to a large extent, are laying aside the ridiculous and even the supposedly sublime educational stumbling blocks in favor of job-related training.

Then, too, we are seeing experimental educational procedures in the colleges and universities that are tending to shorten the traditional four-year curriculum. Such breakthroughs are more than welcome, but tantalizingly slow in surfacing and actualizing.

NEUROSIS AND LOSS OF FREEDOM

Mowrer[3] has succinctly distinguished between normal anxiety and neurotic anxiety. Normal anxiety is the result of frustration, the source of which is known to the sufferer. For instance, we can be anxious about our financial status and do something about it. On the other hand, neurotic anxiety is that feeling of frustration, apprehension, and helplessness, the cause of which is out of awareness; therefore, we cannot attack it.

This neurotic anxiety invariably causes us to narrow our worlds, shutting out perhaps a majority of our possible experiences, leaving only experiences we judge we can handle without having our worlds blow up in our faces. Thus, we lose a part of our worlds and much of our freedom when we are faced with neurotic anxiety. We must defend against the intrusion of new ideas, new thoughts, some of which might shake us up. We have lost our worlds (the fullness of its experiential possibilities), and therewith we have lost ourselves. Freedom being gone, our search is blunted.

Whatever Freudian thought may have done for us or to us, we do recognize that these theorists were correct when they suggested that in neurosis man most of all fears himself. He is afraid of many things, but most of all, his own impulses. These he knows he cannot handle. The base fear of the neurotic is that he might lose control. Such a man is both afraid *for* himself and afraid *of* himself. He is fearful that he might, under the stress of his anxiety, have a heart attack, an ulcer, or some other supposedly irreversible breakdown of his body. The fear of mental collapse is even more severe. Most of all, however, he becomes obsessed with what he might do, i.e., he might destroy himself or a loved one, or he might run amok revealing himself as at least a temporary lunatic. There isn't much freedom in the world of the deeply neurotic person. He may hold his world together, sometimes with the help of drugs, but he is running scared every minute.

Many psychologists have used the concept of wholeness to describe the person free from crippling neuroses. In brief, paraphrasing Kenniston,[4] this suggests that a person must have a capacity for openness, a sensitivity and responsiveness to the world around him, a freedom born of a happy union of his deepest passions and the demands of society upon him. He is capable of commitment, abandon without fear of self-annihilation, wholeheartedness, and passionate concern—and all this with an ethical sense which guides rather than tyrannizes.

THE FREEDOM TO SEARCH FOR MEANING

The most important thing in this world for the individual is meaning for his existence. Frankl[5] has postulated a will to meaning suggesting that the Western world at least is suffering from living in an "existential vacuum."

For Frankl, meaning is different for every person—it differs from man to man and with a certain person from hour to hour. Meaning of a man's existence, for Frankl, is not something he invents but something he finds. People search for meaning in causes, crusades, service, and actions ad infinitum. This search often becomes a function of religious idealism as usually identified. But in a world where the sacred and the secular are becoming increasingly difficult to differentiate, we cannot easily hold to this distinction.

It is easy to adopt the concept of self-actualization so central in the works of Horney, Maslow, Rogers, and others. In this view, meaning comes to the individual through actualizing the self—that is, moving always forward toward greater achievement and fulfillment of the potential we envision within ourselves. Within the Christian view, this becoming may be seen as a growth toward Christ-likeness.

If the self-actualization theorists could be faulted, it would be in that they speak rather glibly about individual self-actualization without due attention being given to the actualization of society. Not that they are unaware that the individual must actualize in society—indeed, they are extremely verbose on that issue. The point is that any effort to self-actualize in an adaptation process to the society that *is* does not open the range of freedoms that would come by way of changing the society; that is, actualizing the society in a direction that would foster individual growth. Admittedly, it is something of the chicken-and-the-egg problem.

Howbeit, we should recognize that social institutions could be changed, too. Despair is rampant in our time as postmiddle-age people, in particular, look upon a world gone mad and find themselves trapped in a cultural process over which they have no power of control. Youth is becoming even more alienated for the same reasons. It is a conflicting reality that the older wish to regress while youth demands progress, even if such progress must be rambunctious, ebullient, and in many cases overreactive. For the young, anything is better than regression or status quo. Actualization is clearly not a one-way street; the culture, too, needs actualization to fit the needs of the evolving, embryonic individual.

Kenniston[6] refers to this being locked in to a social system that regards its institutions as unchangeable as the "psycho-social vise." In order to search for meaning, the individual must project himself into the self-actualization trajectory; but he must also break the psychosocial vise that dictates the style of freedom he could possibly achieve. In this sense, society is not sacrosanct. Institutions may be changed to more nearly fit the aspirational trajectory of men in motion, moving toward actualization.

In a sense, perhaps, it would be easier for a moving object (man) to reach adaptation with an immobile object (society). With both man and society moving, it might be argued that a goodness-of-fit would be even more difficult. Perhaps so, but would not the rewards be more than worth the extra effort? What is the benefit if one changes his perception of self and is forced to accept his entrapment in a static society?

As a case in point of the capability of institutions to change, one needs only to look at the Catholic church as presented in bold relief by former priest James Kavanaugh.[7] Here is an institution that "can know the freedom that is love and not flounder in the conformity which is fear." Or at least *that* represents the longing of James Kavanaugh. Not that other churches are greatly different—the point is that institutions of all types—church, family, school, ad infinitum— can and must be changed if individual freedom is to be actualized.

MEANING AND IDENTITY

Meaning is the *raison d'être* for all of us. Identity is the self-image each of us develops as we pursue our meanings; identity is *the* big goal for all of us. Finding out just who we are, and working toward the ideal self we might become, sustains each of us. Again the young have more zest for answering the question, "Who am I?" As one becomes older, he takes the best partial answer he can derive to that question and learns to accept the who he *has become* with less and less investment in the continuation of the becoming. Being gradually supplants the more action-oriented becoming as one finds himself. In the humanist view, being is the attainment of surer identity and the acceptance of that identity. In the religious view, being is more a reaching toward an at-oneness with the Creator, with God, with Being-Itself, or with the source of our being.

But the identity problem is becoming more and more difficult for all of us. When the pioneer American carved his small farm from the wilderness, constantly protecting his family from Indians, etc., he had little trouble knowing who he was, little trouble with identity.

Technology, as a means of aiding identity, has turned out to be a mixed blessing. Many years ago sociologist David Reisman[8] described the compulsivity of the American worker toward productivity as causing "other-directedness," resulting in alienation, particularly from a sense of selfhood (inner directedness). More recently Erich Fromm,[9] in *Man For Himself,* describes man's power over matter and his "powerlessness in his individual life." Man has been socialized to need what the system creates and Americans, at least, do not know how to live in peace with the time-on-our-hands type of freedom that comes from less hours being given to necessary work. Thus, identity, in terms of things and in terms of work, has diminished to the point that while man has almost everything, he is beginning to discover that he *is* nothing.

All of this suggests strongly that man must seek his identity not in his capacity to have, but in his capacity and commitment of what he does. Thus his being is encompassed in his doing. Glasser[10] has written in his book *The Identity Society* that man is in process of seeking roles rather than goals, meaning that man is more and more investing his sense of worth in what he does than in the money he makes in doing. Erikson[11] makes a strong point of the identity confusion of youth who have so many choices and alternatives that they have difficulty in finding themselves. It may be that when society permits one to gratify prestige needs through doing rather than having, this identity confusion may not be so severe. At least we may be assured at this point that technology has given us a spurious freedom and that we must search beyond technology for identity both in the meaningfulness of our acts and the meaningfulness of being ourselves.

Youth especially face identity problems of great force. In May's[12] terminology, they are "nonentities in an anonymous world." They are increasingly depersonalized. They are numbers on an IBM card. Small wonder that so many become unmotivated and apathetic. They are in process of losing their identity or, in some cases, they simply exist in limbo so far as finding their identities is concerned. They "just can't take hold" as Biff said in *The Death of a Salesman*.[13] Their freedom to search is blunted. But they survive. Too many of them just *exist;* they certainly do not achieve the good life that Aristotle and Christ spoke about.

The Greek maxim "know yourself" has more and more become a necessity. And this necessity demands search, search demands freedom, and freedom is sometimes frightening. To find meaning and then to find identity requires what Tillich[14] has called "the courage to be." Without this search, without this forward movement, the young person feels especially lost, his feeling of worth threatened.

Youth cannot live in stalemate; he can live only as he is permitted, yes, encouraged to search for meaning. If our society and our educational system make this search impossible for him, he cannot survive. If he cannot survive, the world cannot survive either.

Man will not live where he has no meaning as a person. Tournier[15] has made that very clear in his *The Meaning of Persons.* Too many chapters in too many histories of nations have proved that. Clinical evidence suggests that even tiny babies must feel they have reason for being alive evidenced for them through their mother's nurture. Without this feeling, they just stare at the ceiling and die.

THE FREEDOM FROM SEARCHING

Many persons move into the later stages of life still very active mentally, still seeking answers, continuing the process of becoming, extending their beings. But others reach the downhill stage where, according to their own desires, they are content to coast. The active search seems beyond their capacities or desires. Freedom for these is to be allowed to discontinue the search, to live in the context of acquired identities and past accomplishments. For still others, the search continues, but at a lesser pace.

There are many persons who reach a no-further-search-for-meanings stage early in life. Some of these have found such rich meaning for themselves that they do not think it necessary to search further. Many mothers are like this during childbearing and child-rearing years. Some take up the search again when this overpowering sense of meaning begins to break up with the family leaving home. Other parents sink into a quagmire of self-pity, believing their days of meaning and usefulness are gone forever. Most parents may expect to have a diminished sense of purpose and meaning when the children are gone, but the healthy person will build for himself new meanings in work and creative endeavor. This is the better way, of course.

Chapter Ten
Freedom
and Openness

Openness to experience and concepts of freedom and dignity have much in common. It is clear that man has tended, in many instances, to pull his world close around him protectively therewith blunting the possibility of his thrust for meaning. This protective gesture of enclosing oneself into a relatively small life space is an outstanding symptom of the neurotic who is afraid of his own impulses. This is also a tendency of persons who live under strong authoritarian and legalistic (moralistic) influences. Moreover, all of us yield to the restriction of our worlds of experience out of common, everyday fear—fear of the unknown, sometimes fear attendant upon acknowledged risk, and most often perhaps fear of emotions. Skydiving may be relatively safe, but most of us do not yet quite relish the thought of it. It would be just too much of a thrill—too exciting.

Over against this tendency to control our life spaces, we have a reactive desire to experience everything. It is a conflict we shall have to live with to some extent. However, it has been noted by a number of psychologists that openness is a quality displayed by the person who has undergone what was deemed successful psychotherapy. Rogers[1] in his classic *On Becoming a Person*, suggests that openness is the "opposite of defensiveness. . . . He (client) is able to take in the evidence of a new situation, *as it is*, rather than distorting it to fit a pattern which he already holds."

Maslow,[2] in his *Toward a Psychology of Being*, puts it this way: "We grow forward when the delights of growth and anxieties of safety are greater than the anxieties of growth and the delights of safety. Among the objectively describable and measurable characteristics of the healthy human specimen are . . . more openness to experience."

THE BENEFITS OF OPENNESS

Having an enlarged freedom and being open to experience brings the possibility of gain to the person. In whatever manner such expansiveness may be achieved—through psychotherapy, meditation, religious experience, inspiration, or instruction—it has many values. One of these is an enlargement of possible joys one may find in his universe.

Man has always been aware that there are individual differences in perceptual awareness. The poets seemingly can see more beauty in a sunset, a rose, or even a snail on a thornbush than the average man is able to see. And through the creativeness of poetry, the world of beautiful experience has been opened to the nonseeing, again, in a relative sense. But greater awareness does not always bring joy, of course. We may speculate that each man was born with a greater capability of awareness than he maintains at a given stage in his life cycle. To a large extent, our capacity for awareness has been trained (or frightened) out of us.

THE BENEFITS OF TRUSTING IN ONE'S ORGANISM

The person who has been made relatively whole through psychotherapy or other redemptive experiences regains or acquires a sense of trust in his organism. Again, we are indebted to Rogers[3] for making this point so clear, "the person increasingly discovers that his own organism is trustworthy, that it is a suitable instrument for discovering the most satisfying behavior in each immediate situation." This is certainly a valuable by-product of the freedom to experience. It must not, of course, be considered an absolute. Obviously, a person who has a bad heart and knows it, cannot trust his organism to climb a mountain. Obviously, too, the human organism was made to accommodate itself without assistance only to the most optimum of the earth's conditions. Only a few points on the globe permit joyful existing without some form of life-support system such as air-conditioning or heating.

Actually, the trust one has in his organism is couched in the basic belief that the organism as ordered is adaptable; that the input of stimulation, properly assimilated and experienced, can bring relative joy; and that the organism (in cybernetic terms) is equipped with feedback capabilities to the end that actions based upon freedom within the context of calculated risks may quickly be reordered. Being open to most of our possible experiences results in self-confidence that we may handle our worlds and not be manhandled by them. As Rogers[4] puts it, "Consciousness, instead of being the watchdog over a dangerous and unpredictable lot of impulses, of which few can be permitted to see the light of day, becomes the comfortable inhabitant of a society of impulses and feelings and thoughts, which are discovered to be very satisfactorily self-governing when not fearfully guarded."

We should not allow ourselves to be persuaded that the concept of openness to experience must occur in some profound or even dramatic way. Each of us daily, and almost hourly, gives consent to this ideal as we attempt to stimulate our organisms that we may be more alert, wide-awake, sociable, and receptive. We take our coffee in the morning and perhaps intermittently all through the day in order to get that little lift that enlarges our openness to experience. Perhaps we smoke cigarettes and consume alcohol for the same reason, not always with the desired results. Nevertheless, we are constantly working with our organisms, trying to sharpen our sensors and our reflexors. Certain drug stimulation projects us from the ordinary with dramatic impact. Our use of less potent drugs accomplishes similar results less dramatically, but with reasonable efficiency. All forms of opening oneself to experience enhance the capabilities of the organism, capabilities which are a part of racial heredity.

And, for the most part, these stimulants serve us very well. We are made more open to our experiences, our efficiencies are maximized, and our joys of living are increased. Of course, too much even of a good thing may turn out to be bad.

THE QUESTIONABLE ASPECTS OF OPENNESS

The idea of a burned-out, runaway machine is common; the idea of a burned-out human organism is certainly tenable. Certain gasoline engines are built for a certain work load, a certain rpm. They are sometimes equipped with governors to see that this rpm factor is not exceeded. If the governor fails, the engine runs away and soon destroys itself.

The human organism, similarly, was constructed for certain inputs of experience and stimulation. It is greatly adaptable, but its capacity is limited. According to the psychological theory of the general-adaptation syndrome, the organism will eventually succumb to stresses which continue too long. The final stage is the stage of exhaustion; the organism cannot resist any longer. Physical death follows the stage of exhaustion. Admittedly, this theory was propounded to handle the concepts of stress rather than the concepts of enriched experience. But, then, experiences that are more than the organism can withstand, even highly exciting and pleasurable ones, may have the same effect on the organism. Toffler's exciting book *Future Shock*[5] is stark testimony to the possible hurtful effects of too much change on the human organism.

Psychedelic drugs, especially LSD, have been heralded as mind-expanders. Not all persons take LSD for the same reasons, of course, but drug cults are springing up all around. It behooves us to think wisely concerning the possible effects of the psychedelic drugs, which are purported to expand the powers of experience far beyond the ordinary, possibly far beyond the capacity of the human organism to endure. We are not on solid ground in this discussion as the controversy rages on; yet rather unavoidable realities seem to be emerging relating to the users of certain potent drugs, among which are LSD and mescaline.

In the first place, it is unavoidably true that some individuals who take mind-expanding drugs experience breakdowns, which are largely irreversible. These may be described as psychotic breaks or as nervous breakdowns. We would be justified in suspecting that the people who have these horribly bad trips, never to be the same again, are the brittle people who are quite inhibited in ordinary life, who might be described as neurotic, and who are terribly afraid to let go. They are experiencing all of the world they can tolerate even without mind-expansion.

Certainly, the number of these who suffer severe mental crises under drugs is relatively few, but since the damage done them is so horribly severe, we cannot pass it off lightly. Many people say they experience only good trips, and that they can learn how to make the trips better and last longer. For these, we might propose that they are transported out of their dull, mundane worlds into a heightened experience where openness is at its greatest. They experience things outside the capacity of anyone not chemically motivated. Perhaps the mystics, the transcendental meditators may be able, through many years of practice, to approximate this euphoric experience. As Jourard[6] says, it may take the mystic twenty years to achieve what the psychedelic adventurer accomplishes in twenty minutes at a cost of twenty cents.

And what is this experience like? Braden,[7] who interviewed many tripsters and then took mescaline himself, makes these points concerning the nature of the good trip: "(1) The sense of self or personal ego is utterly lost. . . . As for identity, it is not really lost. On the contrary, it is found; it is expanded to include all that is seen and all that is not seen. . . . The subject is somehow united with the Ground of his Being, with the life force that has created the visible world. . . . He is one again with the universe, the eternal, the Absolute; (2) Time stops. Or in any case, it ceases to be important. . . . The subject is content to exist in the moment—in the here and now; (3) Words lose all meaning. . . . An object represents only that which it is. . . . But thing-in-itself perception is beyond all language. It is in fact, the antithesis of language, which is the real cause of our normal inability to see the thing-in-itself; (4) There are no dualities. . . . As a result the world is just as it should be. It is perfect, beautiful. . . . It is transfigured, and it requires no meaning beyond the fact of its own existence; (5) The subject feels he knows, essentially, everything there is to know. He knows ultimate truth. And what's more, he knows that he knows it."

This account of the good trip sounds exciting. One no longer wonders why the drug cultists think of their way of life as a religion. It has all the markings of the great religions. It is disconcerting that this religious experience either *is* chemical or that it is set in motion by chemicals. Whatever else we may say or believe about psychedelic experience, it delivers to the person capable of taking the good trip an openness to experience which at first glance seems quite rewarding. It is a defendable practice for some—at least many vehemently defend it. It is probable that the ones who report these wonderful experiences are not telling all; it is possible that the person who typically has a good trip does not always do so.

It is possible that the consequences for the person who always experiences a good trip may be hurtful in the final analysis, too. In his experience with mescaline, Braden[8] received the unmistakable impression that he was experiencing beyond the intended point human beings are supposed to

118

experience. "Oh, God, we're not supposed to look at this. Not now. Maybe in a million years, or a billion years or ten billion years. But not now, not yet." Braden admits that his reactions may have come from his childhood experiences along with what he had been taught.

But beyond the type of fright Braden expresses, we must ask ourselves the question: is a temporary escape from the capsule via psychedelic drugs beneficial for the person who neither has a bad trip resulting in suicide or psychosis nor a frightening feeling that he is entering where angels would not dare to tread? We must remember that experiences must be calculated and evaluated against the entire spectrum of life as it must reasonably be lived on this earth at this time. In other words, it might be different later, but what about now for you and for me? What happens when the subject returns from his trip, when he is forced by circumstances to return to the humdrum world of wife and children to be fed, of jobs to be done, of the ridiculous but unavoidable requirements of the ambiguous world in which we live? Can he stand it as it is and as it must be for a long while to come? Evidence is pouring in that he cannot. He cannot take it any longer—existence prior to his psychedelic experiences seemed like a nightmare, but after the good trip it seems like hell. No, he must learn to live with his nightmare, attack his problems realistically, or he must cop-out. He must join the hippie culture, denouncing the world of struggle with materialistic values. He must find a new capsule in which to crawl and hide.

OPENNESS AND ACCEPTANCE

Our culture has developed a hurtful internal conflict which seems to be the result of an uncomfortable admixture of the rugged individualism and stoicism of frontier days with our modern urban affluent society wherein interdependence of persons is more and more necessary. We still want to adhere to the old adage of standing on your own two feet, a self-discipline which was absolutely necessary for survival in earlier days. On the other hand, living closer together as we now must, we are urged to get help when we need it, and we have come to realize with John Donne[9] that "no man is an island."

It seems that for most persons this mixing of values in the modern situation has resulted in a fear of being known by our fellows and therewith a lack of openness with each other. As Leona Tyler[10] has suggested, a person does not really want to be understood until he first feels that he is accepted.

The matter of accepting the client in counseling is of prime importance. In everyday human relationships, the fear of not being accepted has driven many of us underground. We are hiding our true selves and our true feelings behind a facade of uneasy bravado. The need to defend ourselves against what our fellows might think of us has made openness virtually impossible for many.

In his *Becoming a Person,* Rogers[11] puts it this way: "He (client) discovers how much of his life is guided by what he thinks he *should* be, not by what he is. Often he discovers that he exists only in response to the demands of others, that he seems to have no self of his own, that he is only trying to think, feel, and behave in a way that others believe he *ought* to think, feel, and behave."

There is absolutely no doubt that our fears of the judgments of our fellows have kept us from being free. Openness has been disallowed for fear of criticism. We cannot say with assurance that these fears are unfounded. Indeed, in many cases it is all too true that to be open with one's fellows would be to lose friends, prestige, and status. Although Jesus strongly urged that we bear one another's burdens, we have come a long way from that in the modern age. We each fear the judgment of the others and have lost our freedom to be who we are. We seemingly must at least to some extent be what we think our fellows would approve. The only self we know is the looking-glass self so well described by Cooley.[12]

One dare not suggest that it would be best just to let go and let be. True, we would probably be pleasantly surprised at how much acceptance we would receive from some; but we would have to face the prospect, if not the reality, of rejection by some others.

In his book, *The New Group Therapy,* Mowrer[13] has expressed these ideas rather fully. Both in the individual counseling situation and in group therapy he has suggested that people should come out from behind their masks and show themselves to each other. Mowrer firmly believes that the fruits of the effort are worth the risks, at least within the therapeutic community.

We may at least hope that we are entering into an age of enlightenment where each of us may regain our freedom to be and to show ourselves complete with all of our socially determined shortcomings. Only then shall we be able to achieve the openness so necessary to the discovery of self and the practical experience of a more refined freedom and dignity.

Chapter Eleven

Making Contact: The Affirmation of Human Worth

Many persons are prone to associate freedom with seclusion. True, much can be said in favor of getting away far from the madding crowd, there to contemplate and rest from the rigors of human associations. For some, this means absolute seclusion, such as Henry David Thoreau seemed to achieve at Walden Pond; for most, it is a relative seclusion such as one would experience on a sandy beach with a single companion, perhaps a romantic interest.

The freedom of isolation, even total isolation, appeals to most of us. We tend to suspect, however, that such isolation would really not be bearable for long. Experiments ad infinitum on sensory deprivation show high levels of stress and many mental anomalies among subjects. Solitary exploration of one's being over long periods is neither comforting nor efficient for the most part. Thoreau[1] wrote from Walden Pond, ". . . it is easier to sail many thousand miles through cold and storm and cannibals, than it is to explore the private sea, the Atlantic and Pacific Ocean of one's being alone." And isolation always forces one into the storms of Thoreau's private sea. We can never *escape ourselves;* and so, solitude turns out to be a false freedom.

Although the private sea is frightening, it is probable that man must experience himself in loneliness and isolation before he can truly grasp the deepest meanings of his existence. Every person, says Moustakas,[2] needs the growth-inducing, deepening values of a genuine, vital, lonely experience. Only through at least an occasional experience of loneliness can a person maintain a truthful self-identity and possess the deepest possible sensitivities and awareness of self and others.

However, man exists primarily in human contact. The presence of others is, for the most part, a definite asset to freedom-seeking, to self-knowledge, to the "knowing thyself" of the Greek maxim. It is clear that the first line of adaptation to one's world is adaptation to oneself. This is the very human problem of identity, so central to man's possible sense of equanimity. But one must have the company of another in order to have a mirror in which to look at oneself. True, not all persons are faithful mirrors; but then, any mirror is better than none at all. There are several aspects of this human help to self-understanding.

In the first place, expanding one's experience of his world is frightening for most; the quieting effect of sharing untested freedoms both of thought and of action makes sorties into the unknown possible. Further than this, it is helpful to have someone at hand to assist in the interpretation of experiences. It is perhaps for this reason that few people smoke marijuana or take LSD alone.

Reality testing is one aspect of the need for companionship in the evaluation of new experiences. One asks another to confirm him in his experience. "Am I right in thinking that cloud formation looks like a genie?" "Do you feel as I do that Professor X is putting me down?"

"Yes, of course, I see what you see. But from my point of view. . . ."

No sunrise is so beautiful as one in the experience of which you can say to another, "See those colors over there—isn't that beautiful?"

"Yes, very beautiful!"

It goes without saying that the more at one, the more communicative these persons are, the more each will contribute to the freedom and the fullness of experience of the other.

THE FREEDOM TO BECOME

There is no becoming in the fullest extent except in the confirmative evaluation of others around us. True, no man can be all things to all people, but each of us is constantly in the act of being and becoming in the eyes of significant others.

The creative experience, which is the essence of freedom at its best, can be accentuated and implemented by other persons. One creates almost always in order that another (or many others) might approve. The artist paints with inspiration because he envisions the creation of his hands through the reactions of others, perhaps of his most beloved. Without the confirmation and acclaim of significant others, most artists become depressed, unable to produce.

The youth of our age seem intent on promoting a new and radically different type of brotherhood. True, they are confused and confounded by many facets of the ambiguous world in which they live. But one thing has been made clear by the pop-music festivals: these young people somehow have developed in the midst of a strongly legalized and moralized society not only a rebellion but a conviction that people are important. They are the epitome of the philosophy "live and let live." They share, they relate, and, in their own strange way (strange to their parents), they love one another.

Freedom and being oneself are strong points in the radical-youth philosophy that is emerging. That freedom and being oneself find expression in nudity and in drug use (perhaps abuse) is disturbing to many, young as well as old. It is undoubtedly true that many youthful aberrations of behavior must be curbed for the good of the many; but to discerning individuals there is a ray of hope in that the human quality of love and sharing are still operating and apparent within these youth groups and among members of the older generation who have responded to critical needs brought about by these massive in-gatherings.

The slogan "make love not war" is usually accredited to the hippie culture. In the efforts of the hippies to embellish the concept of love, we may see some disturbing ambiguities. On the other hand, these people are bringing us into sharp confrontation with the reality of how we have let the concept of love slip away from us in a world of materialistic valuing. To be free is not only to be free from hate but to be free to (toward) love in all of its many ramifications.

In the early '70s, there were a number of evangelists for a revolution of personal values and of styles of consciousness. Among the most noted of these is the Consciousness III life-style suggested by Charles Reich in his *Greening of America.* [3] "There is a revolution coming. It will originate with the individual and with culture. . . . This is the revolution of the new generation . . . the individual is free to build his own philosophy and values, his own life-style, and his own culture from a new beginning."

Reich sees marijuana as the truth serum that expands the understanding of youth, helping them to see behind the facades thrown up by their elders and permitting them to break with the tradition of Consciousness II, which for Reich is the epitome of everything bad that the technocratic society, the corporate state, and bigoted, legalistic religion have foisted upon a people rendered unaware because of their affluential greed and their needs within the competitive world of achievement. The realities of Reich's views of the revolution are being examined and reexamined. There is no doubt that part of what Reich says is actually happening. There is little doubt that his book will help it happen. On the other hand, it is probable that he poses as a guru teaching propositions that will not necessarily ever become truly viable or operable.

Such revolutions as we are experiencing have brought some strange situations. On the one hand, there has been a leap to the East by many youth who are seeking meanings from the mystics; on another hand, there has been a renewal of interest in Marxism and in Maoism. Another subrevolution has brought back the teachings and reconfirmations of the Christian faith and while this movement in itself seems not too disparate from the make-love-not-war slogans of the young, the forms in which the new Christianity are in many cases being presented bring out the worst rather than the best of Christian applications to the human potential movement. In this vein, Revel[4] has contributed another revolutionary format in his *Without Marx or Jesus.*

THE POWER OF LOVE

The human relationship of love is, at its best, the epitome of everything desirable for the enhancement of freedom for one person by the other. If one human loves another, he will surely be constantly striving to aid the fullest possible experience of the other. Through feedback, one human is able to let the other see himself in the growth experience more fully. Thus, the individual may experience a greater freedom to become more and more completely what he has the potential for becoming. The lover brings out the best in the beloved, for the essence of love is wishing the best (widest possible span of comfortable freedoms) for the beloved. The love relationship which does not foster forward growth in freedom to experience for the beloved should be reexamined. Marriage counselors typically cue in on the blockages to this type of expanding experiencing in the marriage relationship.

This concept relates the unselfish act of love within the sexual context. One partner feels complete fulfillment only when he has brought pleasure to the other. Oriental literature is filled with examples of the aging wife who, through her love of her husband, secures for him a young handmaiden who is needed by the husband as a stimulant for his continued freedom and indulgence in sexual expression. While this is a culturally derived practice not yet transmitted to the American scene, it does illustrate the point that true love desires the fullest possible growth toward potential with whatever attendant freedoms are required for the beloved.

The husband and wife in the context of a good love relationship cannot achieve fullness or wholeness without the support, encouragement, and unstinting devotion of the other. This admittedly is stated idealistically and, pragmatically, love relationships fall short of this ideal because of attendant frustration of one kind or another. Still the ideal is there.

HUMAN RELATIONSHIPS AND BARGAINING

Actually, the typical human relationship within and without the marriage experience is one of bargaining. We are, in effect, saying to one another, "You help me to become, and I'll help you." With this comes the need for conforming behavior, for we cannot all have our individual ways at one and the same time.

We conform in order to gain acceptance, therewith gaining support for our own growth process. Conformity is more comfortable than uncomfortable for most of the people most of the time. Obviously, it is not comfortable for the rebel.

We are able to see, however, that the rebel is likely to seek community of some sort. Thus, the hippie culture has developed. And it is unavoidably true that out of a group of nonconforming rebels comes a community in which the conformity principle again begins to operate. Yes, misery loves company; but beyond that, people need people because they cannot grow outside the human environment. We *will conform* for the reason that it is a secure position—we must have company in our valuing process. As a matter of fact, we will knuckle down under values we strongly resist in order to achieve the comforts of conformity.

Conformity in and of itself may accentuate or negate feelings of freedom. American youth, especially, are experiencing a deep sense of alienation. While affluence and technology should reasonably have brought us more peace, contentment, and freedom, it seems that quite the opposite has occurred. The crucial factor in the attendant alienation (not exclusively the generational conflict) is the growing bankruptcy of technological values and visions. Kenniston[5] calls for a transformation "to define a new vision of a society whose values transcend technology." In short, he sees commitment as the key concept in this new society. The implication is conformity with deep and sustained commitment to a new set of values in society—values that bring about technology used for "truly human purposes." This concept is in opposition to a regressive return to intact community where Kenniston feels the individual has been and will be (if communitarian living returns in force) absorbed.

Many others do not agree that communitarian living would rob the individual of his individuality and freedom. Communitarians are not *all* simply suggesting a return to primitivism for idyllic or romantic reasons—although a return to the land with a possibility of enrichment through growing one's own food may definitely and redemptively restore a person to a desirable type of unity with sources. Communitarian life in the main is cooperative rather than competitive; and the typical communal life-style in general does allow for the expression of individual needs and feelings. Communitarian living is indulged as a permanent life style by relatively few, while a larger number of people do achieve some release of the pent-up feeling concomitant with the rat-race society by occasionally partaking of the communal style. Most Americans will remain content to obtain their organic foods at the supermarket where the eminence of fraud is less threatening than dirt under the fingernails.

REVEALING AND HIDING ONESELF

Sadly, man does not always reveal himself to his fellow; and because of this, the possibilities of growth in every relationship are thwarted. Jourard[6] speaks of the encounter that mystifies and the encounter that is transparent. He refers to the transparent encounter as dialogue.

A great deal of emphasis is being placed in the context of group psychotherapy on people's need to stop mystifying one another. It is postulated that man has a fear and distrust of one another, nurtured by the need to defend himself against the expected judgment of others. In his concept of Integrity Therapy, Mowrer[7] emphasizes that man needs to come out of hiding, to share himself with others and receive the benefits of acceptance and confirmation. Hiding out, for Mowrer, is tantamount to a state of mental frustration and illness. Honesty with one another would lessen many of our mental stresses wherein we are seeing the other person as threatening.

Buber[8] has centralized his thinking on the hope that man may see his fellow as a person rather than an object. The I-Thou relationship indicates one person seeing another as a fully acceptable human, while the I-It relationship is one person seeing the other as an object to be used.

Only as we are willing to show ourselves to the other honestly can we be accepted and confirmed as worthy by the other. This requires a feeling of trust and goodwill each toward the other. It is still a somewhat idealistic concept, of course. But it can be attained. Studies in controlled group therapy are pointing the way to the possibility of growth-enhancing dialogue between and among persons.

AWAKENING THE CONSCIOUSNESS OF ANOTHER

Each of us is awakened in our consciousness as a process of growth and experience of freedom. From time to time we reach peaks of experience; we are turned on, able to see with astonishing sharpness what we have never been able to see before. The psychedelic drug is an agent said to be capable of turning people on. But according to Jourard, LSD is not the most powerful psychedelic agent. He says the thing which is most powerful in turning men on is the "awakened consciousness of another human being." In other words, *people* are the greatest awakeners, the greatest mind-expanders. But not just any person can serve others this way. Such a person must himself have been liberated from stifling conventionality. Only then can he see what others have been unable to see. Strangely, these people as they have come along in history have been seen as subversives even as are the modern innovators. Because of this (using Jourard's illustration), Socrates received the hemlock and Jesus the cross.[9]

Such gurus are less than plentiful in our world today. As a matter of fact, these outstanding people are scarcely ever recognized as what they are until they have gone on to other rewards. For the most part, they are seen in their own days as false prophets.

But this only goes to show us the power we have in the lives of others. For it is true that each of us may be a wise man to some of the people with whom we come in contact. Whether or not we feel like gurus, *each of us has a following*. It is an humbling thought.

NEW GROUP APPROACHES TO PERSONAL GROWTH

It is now being recognized that many persons have experienced severe bluntings of their abilities to relate to others. Controlled group experiences for these may become laboratories in human relationships in which great personal growth may be achieved, and these groups may set some people free from constricting tendencies to be suspicious of and shy toward others.

Many approaches variously labeled have attempted to bring people out of their shells into a trusting relationship with their fellows. Among these are the so-called encounter groups, marathon therapy, and psychodrama. Each method has its own special emphasis, but all are aimed at bringing new freedom in the human encounter.

At the Esalen Institute at Big Sur, California, concerted efforts are being made to expand human consciousness, especially through group-participation programs. Here, several of the somewhat controversial touch-and-feel workshops are conducted. Through exercises in touch, these persons who are thought of as withdrawn but not sick are made aware that it is all right for people to touch each other. For some, at least, this yields a new sense of freedom in human relationships. Bishop Fulton J. Sheen has emphasized how the sense of touch (principally in conjunction with his visit with African lepers) may reduce prejudicial reactions and sharpen one's sense of human brotherhood.

Other controversial experiments are being conducted in nudity, and the possible liberating effects of going without clothes is being studied. Nudity seems to be becoming more and more part of the scene at the pop festivals, and the youth at least say that being naked makes them feel like "the real me." It is too early to evaluate these efforts and claims. Undoubtedly, there is good in some of them; others are likely to be perpetuated not as an exercise in redemption but as an exercise in sensuousness. But then, freedom and dignity may be served in ways we do not now have the power to comprehend.

FREEDOM AND ACCEPTANCE OF OTHERS

History has made it clear that the men who have had the capacities to awaken the consciousness of others have been men with strong feelings for the welfare of others. They have had strong senses of social justice and of civic responsibilities. They have seen their fellow human beings as pearls of great price.

Prejudice and bigotry are especially stultifying. One cannot claim an enlarged vision, an expanded world view, and maintain a condescending attitude toward his fellowman. Of the many valued freedoms, freedom from hate, prejudice, and bigotry ranks high.

It comes to this: a human being cannot foster much freedom in his fellows if he does not himself have the freedom from a condescending attitude. And it seems abundantly, although not undebatably, clear that an attitude of acceptance of one's fellows stems from a deep and abiding high regard for oneself.

Chapter Twelve
Freedom and the Roles People Play

Many persons play roles that are fashioned by the culture; these are played in recognition of the role expectations developed over the years. Sometimes these role expectations do not take proper cognizance of fast-developing societal changes; thus, the person finds himself the victim of role conflict in that his behavior, while somewhat ordered by culture and society, is not seen in the same way by all the people with whom he must live and work. There is no doubt that role expectations pose a threat to individual freedom and dignity.

It is logical, even imperative, that a person should play his roles in a unique manner. No one reasonably wishes every lawyer, physician, etc., to be exactly alike. That there are limitations of the variants allowable under idiosyncratic role behavior is obvious, and the individual can go only so far without suffering sanctions from the people with whom and for whom he lives and works. For instance, a teacher who tries to play the role in a manner deemed either by his students or by his patrons and administrators as being far out is inviting dismissal. In this example, the fact that the generation gap is calling for a role conflict in which the teacher seeks to serve the students' expectations, while also keeping in good with the administrators and school's patrons, not only causes loss of dignity, but also unbearable frustration with minute-to-minute decisions having to be made.

In short, we all have difficulty maintaining our dignity in the face of expectations from others, whether such expectations follow a generally described cultural role pattern or a peculiar expectation and demand made by one person upon another, as may be the case in a husband-wife relationship. The amount of freedom we are able to maintain is often a function of our abilities to get by with violations of expectations either by subtlety, placating behavior, or cleverness.

EXPECTATIONS PROVIDE SECURITY FOR SOME

Role playing and role expectations are not always robbers of freedom. Actually, many persons find freedom and dignity through knowing what is expected of them. Many people find nearly perfect peace of mind as they live up to the expectations of others. The frustration for these comes, of course, when the expectations are either ambiguous or vary with different people and with the same people from one time to the next.

There are many who, within the context of their jobs, are happy to adopt the attitude, "Just tell me what you want done and I'll do it to please you. Then I'll leave the job and exercise my freedom in the outside world." Many persons see their jobs, while demanding and restricting for so many hours a day, as giving them assets (money) with which to exercise their freedoms when they are not on the job.

ROLES AND GAMES

The roles of husband and wife are freedom robbing and freedom enhancing. No spouse can be as free as he would be in the unmarried state. There are requirements in the role of husband or wife that restrict behavior.

In describing the games people play, Berne[1] describes a game thusly: "Descriptively it [game] is a recurring set of transactions, often repetitious, superficially plausible, with a concealed motivation; or, more colloquially, a series of moves with a snare, or 'gimmick.' . . . Every game, on the other hand, is basically dishonest, and the outcome has a dramatic, as distinct from merely exciting, quality." Many roles (games) are complementary and mutually helpful between the players even if we accept the basically dishonest label.

In his *Games People Play,* Berne[2] describes the "crossed transaction" as causing "most of the social difficulties in the world, whether in marriage, love friendship, or work. . . ."

There is something unavoidably sad about people who play games at one another's expense. In the context of *transactional analysis,* games are not necessarily fun.[3] The most hurtful game is when the two people who are playing the game are hurting one another unconsciously. In Berne's[4] terminology, these games are "played by innocent people engaged in duplex transactions of which they are not fully aware, and which form the most important aspect of social life all over the world."

GAMES THAT ROB DIGNITY

Most of the dignity robbing games occur between two people intimately related in some way. Obviously, married people are most subject to these more or less unconscious involvements, and one or both spouses may lose personal freedom never knowing where or when it happened. Here are some examples based on my files of persons who have consulted me for psychological help.

1. A woman who marries considerably beneath her social and economic station in life will usually tell her husband-to-be, "I couldn't care less that you are considered to be below me in social standing in the community. We love one another and that's all that matters!" After a few years of marriage the situation may develop in which the woman by word and

137

implication reads the rules of the game to the husband like this: "You did awfully well to get a woman of my standing. Moreover, you might not be able to keep me because there are dozens of men who would like to have a chance. So you'd better watch it. Maybe you shouldn't play golf this afternoon, and pay attention to me instead."

2. The healthiest man in the neighborhood could read the rules of the game like this: "You know, of course, that men are falling out like flies all around with heart attacks. Surely you don't want me to have one. The way to avoid it is to have my slippers and supper ready right on time." Chances are, he will complain occasionally about chest pains, watching the wife out of the corner of his eye. He mustn't be upset, no matter how obstreperous he may be.

3. The very real charge of invalidism has been laid most generally to the wife. She gets headaches easily, especially when the husband wants to do something on his own.

4. The male who wants dutiful sex or even perverted sex from his wife lays down the rules this way: "I know that you women are not like us men. I can't expect you to want me as much as I want you. But, you know that the male has to have constant sex stimulation in order to keep active. Otherwise he will come down with prostate trouble. You wouldn't want that on your conscience, now would you?"

5. The thirty-five-year-old bachelor lives with his sixty-year-old mother. She has money, and he is afraid of marriage. This is a mutually satisfying game, yet it stymies the possibilities for freedom for both. The rules go like this: "Since your father died, I have no one to lean on. And, as you know, son, the problems of marriage are severe. Look how your father crucified me. A woman could do that to you." From his side, "Mother you keep doling out the money, and I'll be a good little boy and not get married. I like the loose living this affords anyway—especially since I have a lot of girls interested in me or, at least, in my new sports car. I don't know or care which. And as long as I get it (money) all eventually, old girl. . . ."

EXPECTATIONS AND AMBITIONS OF OTHERS

The young man or woman who has been victimized by the aspirations of parents concerning their vocational goals are constant clients in the counselors' offices. Sometimes this frustration in not being able to plan and implement their own lives drives them to deeper levels of anxiety, and even to mental illness. In his book *The Meaning of Anxiety,* Rollo May[5] writes of the anxiety attendant upon having to conform to what others expect of us.

This is a senseless waste of personhood, yet it is a common denominator of a great many losses of freedom and dignity. Many people are sweating out their lives in vocations and professions that have enslaved them through the imposition of the lost ambitions of parents—ambitions of parents implemented in the lives of their children. Here, indeed, the sins of the fathers are visited upon the children.

SOCIAL ADAPTABILITY AND DIGNITY

In his *Psychology of Self-Esteem,* Nathaniel Branden[6] says, "The notion that mental health is to be equated with social adaptability is worse than false; it is actively dangerous. . . ." It is not difficult to agree with this assessment. At the same time, there is for many a *type of security* in social adaptability, although as Branden says, "There is no *equation* of mental health and social adaptability." Obviously, many persons have developed the capacity for going along with social demands while laughing up their sleeves. For them, conformity is an expedience, and they utilize the values inherent in adaptability to a society to further their own creature comforts while throwing aside the shackles at intervals.

It is summarily not wrong to conform to either social pressures or to personal pressures. It is what happens to the person who conforms that counts. Conformity is not all bad;

and although certain freedoms must be abandoned with conformity, certain others may actually be enhanced.

MULTIPLE ROLES AND ROLE CONFLICT

In his *Becoming a Person* Rogers[7] says: "Below the level of the problem situation about which the individual is complaining—behind the trouble with studies, or wife, or employer, or with his own uncontrollable or bizarre behavior, or with his frightening feelings, lies one central search. It seems to me that at the bottom each person is asking:'Who am I, *really?* How can I get in touch with this real self, underlying all my surface behavior? How can I become myself?' "

These queries, as posed by Rogers, raise still others. Is there indeed a real person, a real self that is being camouflaged by the multiplicity of roles he is being forced to play? Or is it not more likely that such a tenable *real* self *is* a multiplicity of roles, howbeit an admixture which reflects rather accurately the self-concept of the person? If this last position be taken, then it is still realistic to assume that many people have lost their real selves in forced role behaviors which are not in keeping with what the person *could recognize* as his true self. This is more likely the case. It is not that there is a real self aside from the roles he plays, but that the roles he *must* play confuse the identity of the person who is in the context of his real self a constellation of roles compatible with his concept of self.

That modern man is forced to play multiple roles is undebatable. He becomes businessman, father, country-club member, churchman, P.T.A. member, scoutmaster—on and on, ad infinitum. Some of these roles he chooses, others are forced upon him as consequents of initial free choices, still others are forced upon him as expediencies of his making a living for his family, etc. Obviously, he accepts some roles out of a service-oriented life style. We may suspect that other roles are accepted out of a basic compulsivity in the individual or out of a conditioned inability to say no.

The long and short of it is that most of us find ourselves playing a multiplicity of roles, many of which bring us into conflict because the summation of roles is incompatible with any possible identity of ourselves as person, *as who we think we really are.*

The confusion of being so many things to so many people very well may place us in a position of being so involved with projects as to meet ourselves coming back. We would be that busy and frenetic with all these activities; thus we should have lost freedom to be and to do those things which really bring us release, pleasure, and fulfillment. On the other hand, among these many roles we must play in our fast-paced world, there may be some conflicts which cause psychological tension. For instance, the businessman in his dealings with others may be forced to cut corners or drive hard bargains that are not the epitome of a viable expression of love for one's fellowman. But, as a teacher of a Sunday-school class in his church, this man must espouse those acts of brotherly kindness which he is forced to violate in his day-by-day business activities. This is role conflict. Freedom and dignity can be lost by accepting too many roles in the first place and by allowing oneself to become involved in conflicting roles in the second place.

ROLE CONFLICT WITHIN
A SINGLE-ROLE DIMENSION

The social psychologist makes several distinctive uses of the role-conflict idea. As contrasted to the conflict between roles as described above, there is also the conflict within a single role. Kirkpatrick,[8] in his book *The Family: As Process and Institution,* demonstrates this by referring to six separate interpretations of the role of the female college graduate. These are listed as: (1) career-singleness, (2) marriage-maternity homemaking, (3) low-fertility companion, (4) low-fertility-marriage-plus-career, (5) fertile-marriage-plus-full-career. In cases like these, the individual who tries to play two or more of these loosely distinguishable role patterns is inviting conflict with loss of equanimity. It is one thing to know who you are and yet another to decide *who you are going to be.* Failure to make a clear-cut decision as to who you are going to be usually brings the honest and searching question, "Who am I, *really?*" And then, once a person has made the original mistake, he comes to the counselor in an effort to backtrack and find the *real self* which was lost in the melee.

ROLE STRAIN

Still another social-psychological concept is role strain. Role strain seems vested in the social system or subsystem, but has its debilitating effects on the individual. Knapp[9] uses the college professor to illustrate role strain. The typical professor is caught in a number of squeezes. His loyalty to his employer often conflicts with what he thinks he ought to do and say as a function of his academic discipline. He is torn between the publish-or-perish demands and the energies required to be a good teacher. He is expected and really often wishes to be a social creature, but his writing and research force him into an apartness.

Role strain is probably at the base of the ulcer syndrome for the business executive who wants to be kind to people, but his obligations to the stockholders force him to demand more and more from the people he would like to treat humanely. He must make decisions that affect people adversely and the company beneficially. The strain usually tells on the executive sooner or later. The big money he presumably makes hardly compensates for the ulcer he develops. But he is caught on a treadmill and can't get off. Too much is at stake—his pride, the standard of living to which he and his family have become accustomed, his self-concept as a prime mover in the business world. It is at best a vicious circle and he becomes a virtual prisoner to his job.

At first impulse we might say, "To hell with it. Let's all exercise our capacity for freedom and get off these treadmills." But it isn't as easy as that. If we do anything at all, we must choose between freedoms, for to abdicate in favor of one freedom forces us to surrender others. The freedom to drive a Cadillac may be dependent upon a loss of freedom through role strain which is unavoidable if we stay on the job.

Yet man's ingenuity should make it possible for him to solve this problem, to at least have part of his cake while eating the other part. Goode[10] in his article "The Theory of Role Strain," makes several suggestions. Among these is the delegation of more responsibilities to others and the use of secretaries to ward off visitors. Each person must work at the elimination or lessening of role strain in his own way and in the context of the possibilities inherent in his own situation. There is no doubt that something can be done about it. Dignity and freedom are too precious to give up the battle.

Chapter Thirteen

Freedom, Work, and Leisure

Old worlds die hard. A large part of the population of age forty-plus was introduced to a world of scarcity, a world where one worked by the sweat of his brow in order to fight away the wolves. One saved, one hoarded when times and crops were good, for the rainy day was always just around the corner. Today's youth find this hard to understand, for they have never been exposed to scarcity—at least many of them have not—although we do have a severe poverty problem among the disadvantaged. The parents are not at all sure the plenty will last, and most try frantically to teach the young the value of the dollar. The young are realistically wondering if there is any value in the dollar—not only from the point of view of its depreciation under inflation, but in terms of an overriding philosophy which, on the one hand, decries the materialistic obsession of the Western world and, on the other hand, firmly believes that the days of scarcity are gone forever.

Perhaps a world has really died. And there is no possibility of a romantic regression, no turning back. There is absolutely no doubt that a new era has dawned. It has dawned; but man has hardly been able yet to fashion the questions he should be asking, much less the answers to these questions. We are standing upon the threshold of the cybernetics revolution, a revolution that is likely to make the industrial revolution seem insignificant in historical perspective. With the cybernetics revolution, it may really be true that the overriding spectre of scarcity that has shaped man's values for so many centuries will be gone forever.

Cybernetics is a word coined to symbolize a superscience in which machines not only do man's work, but do a large part of his thinking as well. The chief actor in this drama is a thing currently being called a computer—a complex machine capable of handling vast amounts of information and of instantaneously giving answers to queries put to it in the form of programs. Everyone has heard it said that the computers are programmed, that they give out the answers, and that those answers are almost inevitably sure and quick.

It is true—all of it. Computers are mushrooming into wide use in business and industry. They are solving problems, including the problems of space travel, in an unbelievably efficient way. They seem to have ushered in an era when the chief problem will no longer be supply of consumer goods. The problem will be the creation of a society that can be motivated to buy and consume this endless supply of goods which will flow from assembly lines via computerized technology like water from the proverbial miraculous pitcher.

Automation was an in-between state—between the industrial and the cybernetic revolution. Man feared that automation would take away his jobs; the spectre was the push-button factory. But the sociologists and the economists were quick to say no. These machines would make life easier, not jobs more scarce. Men would always be needed to build these machines, to repair the automated machinery, and to push the buttons. We would simply enjoy an expanded freedom and a higher standard of living *with more of everything.* True, they said, the work-week will be cut down, maybe to as little as thirty hours per week for some. But life would go on as before because, after all, man was supreme—the machines can't think.

This viewpoint under cybernetics may turn out to be the world's most cruel joke. For it is now abundantly clear that the machines, aided by computers, do have an intelligence. "No," the wag says, "machines can't think. But they think they can." But it's all too true! The age of automation has gone with the industrial revolution, for now we have the computers to push the buttons of the push-button machine. And where does that leave mere man?

Man is under threat of becoming more "mere" than he ever dreamed possible. Man has always distrusted machines, always feared them. They were imponderable (how many of us really understand the computer today—it's just a word we use for the most part), frightening, always threatening to upend a cherished way of life wherein man was only too happy to be relieved of the sweat of his brow, but not at all sure he wanted to be done out of the work of his hands. In brief, man has always felt diminished by machines. They have made him question his own value, his reason for being in the world. As machines have increased, so has man decreased—in value, that is. Or so man seems to feel.

THE THREAT OF LEISURE

It is now being suggested that man will have at least one-hundred hours of leisure time per week. It is freely conceded also in political as well as in economic circles that larger and larger numbers of uneducated people will require some type of minimum-income support. Under cybernetics the best guess is that the uneducated may work only at "busy-work tasks" with perhaps much more than one hundred hours per week of leisure, while the highly educated may actually work more and more hours. Only the highly educated will be doing meaningful work in terms of keeping the production lines moving.

Man has always seen work paradoxically. On the one hand, he has lost his freedom to the work task. The sweat shops and the rat races have forced man into virtual slavery on the one hand, and organizational-man status on the other. To the one he has lost his time, and to the other his identity. On the other side of the coin, work has been seen as a savior. Man's selfhood has been enhanced in creative endeavor. And even in the most dull and repetitive tasks, man has usually been able to identify with the product. He has been able to immortalize himself with the work of his hands.

Great amounts of leisure are likely to involve mankind in considerable conflict. The behavior and sometimes shortened lives of the retired persons have shown us that man has been conditioned to the value inherent in his work, and suffers not so much a gain in freedom as a loss under enforced leisure. Leisure and boredom must become the horns of our overriding dilemma. Boredom is certain to become the windmill we must attack with quixotic abandon. But what will be our steed; and what will comprise our lance for the attack? In quest of freedom and dignity, we must raise this question; indeed, we *must* have an answer to it before it really maddens us.

Two things may be suggested. First, we must have a renewed concept of personal integrity and worth, and second, we must learn to engage each other in meaningful relationships and dialogue. Fishing and golf will help, but only if we have human companionship, and only if we are able to see ourselves as worthwhile in leisure as well as in work.

Leisure can be the highest form of freedom or it can become a virtual ensalvement depending upon the process of one's growth within the pattern of leisure. Hale and hearty men in a forced retirement are destined to live out their lives in the throes of a loss of meaning.

How lucky the truly creative person will be! Leisure cannot destroy the person who has capabilities of creativity for he may create regardless of what happens to his regimented job. And creating is the highest form of freedom. One can create only in freedom, and creative genius is the highest expression of dignity.

THE EXPLODING TECHNOLOGICAL WORLD

New eras evolve with relative slowness, although everything including profound change comes more quickly now than at any time in man's history. With the first moon walk, it was said that a new age was born. "One small step for man—one giant leap for mankind," said Neil Armstrong. Usually, a new era is heralded in by a specific event, but the new era has been shaping for quite a few years. The impact is no less great, for in the minds of men they emotionally choose to identify the event with the advent.

All is not gloom—it is time for optimism, not pessimism. John Diebold[1] has issued this exhilirating statement, "Each time a major scientific innovation has been made, we find that our own concept of ourselves becomes more profound." Julian Huxley[2] wrote: "The scientific and technical explorations have given the Common Man all over the world a notion of physical possibilities. Thanks to science, the underprivileged are coming to believe that no one need be underfed or chronically diseased, or deprived of the benefits of its technical and practical applications."

It is true—perhaps more dramatically true as an aftermath of man walking on other planets than with any other event, that man perhaps feeling diminished by it all turns back to himself with a renewed zeal to search out his meaning. Man's humanness stands out more starkly against the conquests of technology that threaten his personhood and cause him to react.

After the first moon walk on July 20, 1969, Werner Von Braun, perhaps the greatest scientist of all, issued a statement reflecting not only his God-orientation, but his world view and his view of the nature of man. "God will now be seen as a universal God, not earth-bound," he said. "And man shall turn his thoughts not away from technology, but surely back to his ethical values and a reinvestment in himself as the most supreme of all the creations."[3] These are the things we must be prepared to fight for. These are the questions in which we must invest enough of ourselves to derive the answers. We must be ready not only to affirm but to defend man's freedoms.

In his *Portrait of a Man Standing,* de Madariaga[4] says, "The astounding command over nature that man has been achieving at a growing pace during the last century—a prelude, it would seem, to even more astonishing conquests—augurs a prodigious future for the human being. . . . But we must bow to the facts. This future will not blossom unless quality is saved from quantity, the tree from the cow . . . the spirit of man, while the cow grazes at his feet, will go on for centuries of centuries rising, stretching his arms like tree branches, longing and yearning at least to touch with the tips of his fingers, the buds of its twigs, the blue veil that conceals the mystery."

FIGHTING AGAINST HUMAN CONTROL

Man has a nature that moves him toward freedom. Unfortunately, however, man's freedom is perishable—it can be lost. Freedom certainly *will be* lost when men stop believing that they are free; when they think of themselves as impotent to resist manipulation.

Let's face it. Even with our inner drives for freedom, even with an optimistic view, we are still in much danger of becoming manipulanda at the mercies of a machine-oriented society. This is perhaps more true of the uneducated man who cannot see the dangers until he has already succumbed to them. Herein is a part of the frustration of skilled laborers under unionization. They have been taught to sell their productivity as if it were only a commodity. Surely man should realize more from his labor (time) than money, the symbol of commodity value.

Men may be inspired to believe in their freedom, but their powers of free choice may disappear in an environment that does not permit them to make choices. And never doubt that such an environment is imminent unless we intelligently pit ourselves against it.

We can indeed become boxed in by social patterns in which we, by default, allow so much control of our lives as to leave for us no meaningful autonomy. B.F. Skinner's *Walden Two*[5] depicts a controlled society wherein all except the controllers simply follow the guidelines laid down for them. They eat, sleep, and cohabit according to a plan, a plan which has been worked out by the manipulators to give to the controlled the maximum in good and carefree living. *Walden Two* is a utopian society where every need is humanely taken care of by careful controls. Lip service is even given to a type of autonomy for the inhabitants. But the message gets through; man is living as those in authority (benevolent despots though they be) wish him to live. The controllers of superintelligence plot the real destiny.

The dangers of a controlled society are much greater than we may be able to realize. The works of Ayn Rand depict this idea over and over again. *The Fountainhead*[6] and *Atlas Shrugged*[7] give the sharp picture of man's default of personhood. He defaults because he is overtaken by controls before he knows he is being controlled. The controls are very subtle. Societies become the unmechanical tool that can almost diabolically enslave by a coercion from without—a coercion which perfidiously seems to come from within.

SLAVES OF TECHNOLOGY

In his book *Tangled World,* Roger Shinn[8] says, "... we may note that the affluent economy often manages to thrive by appealing to the worst motives of people rather than their best. The furious flow of products from the factories brings a perverse pressure on people to buy and consume."

The historian Arnold Toynbee[9] says this about advertising: "It has made a fine art out of taking advantage of human silliness. It rams unwanted goods down surfeited throats when two-thirds of all human beings alive are in desperate need of the bare necessities of life." It would not be quite so bad if the people who are being enslaved by technology knew what was happening to them. It is rather amazing that Vance Packard felt the need to write his *Hidden Persuaders*[10] in order that people might know how the advertisers are exploiting human motives which the general public seems not to realize are there to be exploited. We can hope that Ralph Nader is and will continue to be uncontaminated by the interest of any group except the public.

Heidegger, in his *Discourse on Thinking,*[11] graphically describes the nature of man who becomes enslaved by technology: "... the approaching tide of technological revolution in the atomic age could so captivate, bewitch, dazzle, and beguile man that calculative thinking may someday come to be accepted and practiced as the only way of thinking. ... What great danger then might move upon us? Then there might go hand in hand with the greatest ingenuity in calculative planning and inventing indifference toward meditative thinking, total thoughtlessness. And then? Then man would have denied and thrown away his own special nature—that he is a meditative being."

It seems clear that man is in danger of not putting first things first. And why is that? One finds it difficult to imagine a more complex undertaking than the conquest of outer space, the planets, the solar system and beyond, or of inner space, the atom and it's intricacies. But there is a greater mystery; that which man is himself. Is it possible that we are passing up the greater mystery in favor of the lesser because of its profundity, its complexity? Yes, it seems so. Either that or because so many false starts—or, at least, starts which cannot be verified as to their validity—have made us leery of the quest.

Chapter Fourteen
Human Dignity and Youthful Rebellion

Things are not as they should be. Human freedom and dignity are being greatly curtailed because of existing conditions in the establishment—the establishment being identified as institutions ranging from the home to the federal government. Under the guise of a sane approach to economics and human togetherness and all the problems these concepts entail, the home, churches, educational institutions, and government agencies—to name only a few of establishment's functionaires— are exercising controls and proposing authoritative stances affecting the fabric of life in our nation and in the world. These establishment positions are too often a thin veneer of subtle camouflage hiding highly questionable corporate economic gains or special concessions to special groups. Indeed, these facades, which often exalt the causes of truth and justice, become transparent gimmicks when exposed to the penetrating

153

criticisms of rebels, mostly young people whose eyes have not yet become glazed with traditional concepts of what is good and what is right.

Youth is developing an acute sense of discovering adult cover-ups which were probably conceived as honest efforts at justice by the adults who engineered them. It seems safe to say that these engineers could not see and are not seeing the fallacies of their establishment values, but rather, are firmly, albeit sometimes honestly, convinced that they are serving the cause of justice, freedom, and dignity very well indeed.

Take a few cases in point. Giant corporations are espousing a doctrine of benefits to society in the form of products to be desired and jobs to be enjoyed. This sounds very good and commendable—it is, at least, consonant with the concept of private enterprise in a free society. But beneath this seemingly innocent and beneficent exterior, the auto makers, for example, are releasing products that are, as Ralph Nader has said and adequately demonstrated, unsafe at any speed. More than that, the factories are committing environmental violence dialy. In service to what have seemed worthy goals, pollution runs rampant and the gods of materialism reign supreme.

Then, too, colleges and universities in the name of an educated citizenry, are ramming unwanted and unneeded academic jargon into surfeited brains that are likely to be the worse for having this extraneous mass of verbiage and unrelated concepts leading not to productivity, but to confusion, fed into them.

THE PARADOX OF REBELLION

Rebellion, however, can serve two very divergent masters. There was a time when loyalty to cultural institutions and statutory law was seen as automatically good. It is no longer so. But in the spirit of rebellion in which *nothing* is automatically conceded to be good, we are faced with a very dangerous situation. If there are to be no laws, no generally accepted standards by which a majority of citizens are willing to govern themselves, then the only alternatives are chaos and a police state.

It is patently impossible to have everyone doing his own thing. One person's freedom is sure to bring about another person's chaos. *Responsible* action becomes a must. If the freedom becomes license and results in violence, then society will have to respond with violence in the form of strong law enforcement; and the end of that road is surely a police state.

But, on the other hand, rebellion (perhaps even of the violent kind) is surely sometimes necessary. Only through the spirit of rebellion (usually spearheaded by youth) can it be hoped that the inconsistencies of a supposedly informed and benevolent society may be brought to the consciousness of misled but reasonable people. There is summarily no reason for putting up with rules and conditions which make life narrower and less satisfying than it could be.

The moving force behind intelligent rebellion must be an earnest desire to improve the *quality* of life rather than become obssessed with status and possessions. We are surely headed down the wrong road in our society where values have been too long interpreted in terms of possessions and power instead of a relishing of life. That there must be a delicate balancing act between quality and quantity cannot be argued. Establishment's obsessions with getting ahead, entering space, setting feet on the moon, etc., have brought rewards that make life more worth living. Medical discoveries that have controlled poliomyelitis, tuberculosis and the like, have come from research programs which very well could have been written off by rebels as a quantitative waste, wherein certain individuals have enjoyed inequitable personal gains from the expenditure of vast amounts of government money.

The growing spirit of rebellion could either ruin or save us. We *must be* intelligent enough to recognize the differences between constructive and destructive rebellion.

YOUTHFUL EXTREMITIES AND EXCESSES

Among the more frightening spectaculars of the present day are the extreme behaviors of youth. Extremities are everywhere, but they come into sharpest focus in the context of the rock music festivals, Woodstock being the classic example. True, Woodstocks are having a hard time these days, but the spirit is still there.

In a lucid statement, Abbie Hoffman,[1] the yippie leader, and a defendant in the Chicago-seven trial said, "I live in a Woodstock nation. . . . It is a nation of alienated young people. We carry it around with us as a state of mind in the same way the Sioux Indians carried the Sioux nation around with them. It is a nation dedicated to cooperation versus competition."

Many youth are openly flaunting establishment values with expressions of rebellion against not only the economic values of the establishment, but against the values attendant upon doctrinaire religion. Even if we all give assent to situational ethics and the new morality that says nothing is bad or wrong unless someone gets hurt, we simply cannot be unmoved by such excesses as open sexual indulgence, nudity, and drug abuse. True, all of these things are said to be expressed in a nonviolent manner, and they are being done with lip service to freedom. Usually, the legal authorities are coerced to look the other way, ignoring all except the most flagrant violations of statutory law. To a large extent, what have been and still are establishment's codes of decency are passed up with no attempts at control, disparagement, or even discouragement. As a rule, a disturbed but permissive society sets up medical facilities to take care of overdosing from drugs and makes concerted attempts to provide food and sanitation.

Festivals are generally conceded to be mass demonstrations of the values of youth throughout the entire society, although it might be suspected that there is a crowd psychology operating in these gatherings which cause youth to dare a bit beyond what they would ordinarily do on a Saturday night in their home towns. What happens at the festivals is sometimes what youth has done already before, sometimes what they know they *can do* with impunity.

What do all these things mean beyond the raw evidence that youth is in rebellion against the establishment, many of whose values are conceded to be inconsistent and even senseless? Is the freedom of excess and extremity (with these terms defined as rebellion against society's legalized and most commonly accepted standards of conduct) helpful or hurtful to a human dignity in which a vast majority of citizens can live in security and reasonable serenity? The almost unavoidable conclusion is that these acts of rebellion on the part of youth are more damaging than redeeming. Even if, through these behaviors, some reasonable questions of rightness are focused upon the inconsistencies of the establishment, the dangers of these types of behavior sweeping through the nation are too great to ignore. Drug abuse brings muggings as abuse becomes addiction. Sexual promiscuity results in pregnancies, and even with an enlightened view of abortion, there is considerable damage done as long as we continue to live (rightly so or not) with a set of values (even in a transitional sense) which stigmatizes the victim (female) of promiscuous sex.

WHY MARIJUANA?

The greatest puzzlement of all concerning youthful rebellion is their marijuana binge. Why so much pot? At the music festival, it is true that the air is permeated by the smell of it.

We may be certain that the widespread use of marijuana for youth is not the same motivationally speaking as is the use of psychedelic drugs by the drug cultists. Whether marijuana should, in fact, be considered psychedelic is an unanswered question. There is little doubt that it can bring about the effects so often associated with mind expansion, but it is more often either simply euphoric or not effective. Many youth report in confidence that it doesn't really do anything to them or for them. They smoke it because everyone else seems to be doing it, and many put on the effect that they have learned to expect.

No doubt about it—marijuana is the rebellion drug for youth of today. In this sense, it is like the alcohol binges of a few years ago. Some answers we know. Marijuana is relatively cheap. It is illegal, and that makes using it exciting. It is probably not harmful. Interestingly, Charles Reich[2] in *Greening of America,* refers to marijuana as a "truth serum."

Rollo May[3] has called Reich's Consciousness III "an impressionistic painting of the GARDEN OF EDEN . . . for children and not for adults." The important question is whether or not today's youth are continuing to be enchanted about utopian concepts of countercultures. In talking with today's college students, I get the impression that they are not as a group ready to be lured into such proposed revolutions, but are instead moving toward a much more intelligent confrontation with a society which will, as they now seem to believe, continue to follow the free-enterprise format. But they are committed to change, especially as the ongoing system may accommodate to needed social reform.

The use of LSD is on the way down. Why? Probably because youth have become convinced that it truly is harmful in many ways; although blame is currently being placed more on impure LSD. But marijuana is generally thought to be safe unless you get caught. It is also thought to be nonaddictive; but the older generation, including the legal arm of society, violently reacts to its use. And that combination is attractive to youth! There was a time when youth were more skeptical because they had been convinced that marijuana led to the hard stuff. Now they don't believe it. While statistics formulated at some of the federal treatment centers for narcotics addicts show about 75 percent of the addicts started on marijuana, other statistics show that only about 10 percent of those who use marijuana become addicts to heroin or other hard narcotics. That marijuana becomes the open door for hard drugs *for some* is undeniable.

So, although it is a puzzlement why so many young people use marijuana, it may be concluded that marijuana is the choice because it isn't really terribly dangerous (or thought not to be), but that it really does turn the older generation on when the young use it (witness the drastic penalties for possession still existing in some states), whether or not it turns the young person on.

WHAT ARE THESE YOUNG REBELS REALLY THINKING?

One cannot help but wonder what goes on in the minds of these youth. We can do little more than surmise, for even if we ask them, we are not likely to get straight answers. Many of the more sophisticated cite the inconsistencies of the establishment and say that they are rebelling so that society may know how to correct its shortcomings. They say that they will not make concessions to a materialistic society which places its values on *things.* And they say that they are proponents of an all-encompassing love which demands that everyone share whatever they have, including drugs and bodies. Their critics are quick to point out that they eagerly accept the sandwiches proffered and that they often have money to spend and expensive cars to drive—that they don't really believe this bit about materialism, that they want the benefits of a materialistic society while having a great time raising hell about it. Maybe all this is true.

On the other hand, it is more than probable that a majority of these young people really don't know either what they want or what they are rebelling against. They are just going along for the ride—the music is great, the sex is good, and the pot isn't all that bad—it is at least *supposed* to turn you on.

Have these youths really thought through what it would mean if the world accepted their terms? Not having had to work for a living as did their parents during the depression, they may foolishly think that the world is going to be one big handout whether people accept responsibility, work hard, or don't. For them the world has been flowing with the proverbial milk and honey all of their lives. They just may not be mature enough to realize that the honey is a little mixed up with their parents' sweat and tears. But why should they be aware of that—their parents never told them, they only wanted Mary and Johnny to have it good and easy, and not have to work "like we did."

And beyond all that, the parents are possibly so intent on their own freedoms and pleasures that they are more than willing to shell out the money so Johnny can have that car and plenty of gasoline and pot money—just so long as the kid doesn't "get in our hair." So who is being ridiculous? Who is being immature? Aren't we all!

THE CAMPUS SCENE

We may hope that campus rioting has cooled. Still, even with the end of the war, campus violence erupts from time to time. Whenever campus rioting occurs, the police move in to protect public property (either the police of the immediate area, or the national guard). Order must be kept, it cannot be allowed that property be blatantly destroyed. But it is surely probable that the law-enforcement officials who draw the duty of crowd control can hardly be sympathetic to the volatile emotions of the students. Indeed, the students typically taunt the "pigs" and, in some cases, engage in bloody violence in confrontation with them. As deplorable as the Kent State, Jackson State and Baton Rouge (Southern University) events are, it is difficult to place the blame squarely on the shoulders either of law-enforcement groups or of the students.

When conditions of violent rioting occur, it is obvious that crowd psychology will draw students who don't really understand the grievances but who take sides with their peers no matter what the provocations may have been. On the other hand, riots tend to attract nonstudent sympathizers, some of whom really identify with the students, and some of whom are planfully and willfully serving as catalysts to foment a riot.

Realistically, as Shoben[4] concludes, there has been very little evidence to support claims of communist or other subversive instigations of campus riots. There seems to be abundant

160

explanation for student unrest without suggesting subversive conspiracy. This is not to say that the enemies of America may not be beginning to recognize and seize the opportunities that are obvious.

YOUTH ON SOCIAL WELFARE

There is a deeply penetrating disenchantment with the status quo of a society which seems to behave so dispassionately toward the disadvantaged, the poor, the alienated, etc. Many things need to be done about man's inhumanity to man. These young people are hypersensitive. They are recipients of information about society's inequities, inconsistencies, and incongruities via communication channels which put into their immediate consciousnesses events that happen anywhere on this shrinking globe.

If something is not done about these acts of inhumanity, then out of their new life style which places compassion at one end of their valuing process and exploitation at the other end, they react—and they react existentially. They want action, and they want it *now*. A phased withdrawal of troops from any occupied country does not satisfy—we're wrong, let's admit it!

"What's wrong with a society that will allow napalm to be manufactured in the plant across town from the university, an economically based establishment which pays their professors handsome bonuses for research designed to kill more babies?" they ask. And these same professors are virtually stealing from the students whose tuition dollars are siphoned off, not to give the students the education they pay for, but to perpetuate a rotten society.

That the students are often inconsistent in their demands when these demands are evaluated from the point of view of establishment values does nothing except to turn them on even more ferociously against the establishment which values material things more than human life.

STUDENT REVOLUTIONARIES

Admittedly, most students experience a degree of unrest. Most students do not assert their feelings of unrest. Other students, feeling the alienation and helplessness that would ordinarily relegate them to a robot state, react with desperate need to, as Shoben[5] says, "assert their identity as a way of finding it, to upset the workings of what is perceived as an insensate machine . . . a reaction that takes ad hoc forms, depending primarily on tactical considerations of the moment, in its enraged assault on the perceived Establishment."

Most campuses have not as yet experienced demonstrations and certainly not violent confrontations. We have no way of knowing whether the movement will escalate or dwindle. It is certain that some campuses are not ripe for revolution, and that some never will be. Violent and even highly vocal confrontations usually take place on campuses that have a history of liberal stances on many issues.

In most situations where violent confrontations have occurred, it has been discerned that there is a small cadre of revolutionary leadership—usually including some professors in supportive roles—most often fifty or less even at the large universities. The extent to which this cadre is able to commandeer the loyalty of students depends upon events, some of which can be precipitated by the leaders, and some of which simply happen. This cadre typically tries to rally students behind them via mass meetings. The group who publicly display loyalty to the revolutionaries is usually relatively small, perhaps less than five hundred on a university campus of 20,000 students. On the other hand, as was the case at Columbia, as many as one-fifth of the students may support the radical faction, especially where acts of police violence (brutality) have been observed. Most often, students do not wish to disrupt their own educations.

When revolutionary tactics emerge, there again is an intrusion of crowd psychology. Students who otherwise would not participate in a mass meeting may be swept along by the psychology of crowd behavior and participate in burning a building. Their powerlessness finds a means of expression, a means in which individual culpability is obscured.

STUDENT UNREST AND FREEDOM AND DIGNITY

Unquestioning allegiance to a body of rules that restricts life without in any way adding to it is definitely a loss of freedom. For this reason, student unrest is the beginning of a legitimate quest for freedom and dignity. When dissent is expressed in ways that yield reasonable hope of bringing about reasonable changes in a reasonable time, then freedom is being served. Much student unrest is taking these types of constructive directions; and college administrations, although bound by innumerable restraints from the older citizenry, are yielding to student requests and demands for change.

But when an extremist group acts to abolish a rule simply because that rule is disliked, freedom suffers if this action is regarded as a right with impunity. It is usually true that activist groups do not attend in full to the complexities of the issues, and demand an immediate solution to profound problems. In the heat of an agitated confrontation with police or national guardsmen, raw emotion erupts and the cause of freedom and dignity is seldom served.

As is always true in cases of extreme differences, there are protagonists and antagonists. Some strong statements have been made about student revolts. Strong statements are often at least partially true. It is probably true that many of the rioting students are properly classified as "an effete corps of impudent snobs." One might even feel embittered against the students who yield to crowd psychology, sometimes commiting acts of violence. But there is a difference between the calculating perpetrators of violence and those who are swept up in such violent confrontation just because they were there. It is hardly defendable to say to one's son or daughter who has been jailed for being in the wrong place, "You should have been in your dormitory studying and you wouldn't be in jail now."

Youth must be heard, in the interests of ultimately wresting a viable freedom and dignity from a complex welter of conflicting values and goals. Student unrest may easily be seen basically as a generational disagreement in values. If that is what it basically is, then it is not therewith adequately demonstrated that the values of youth should ultimately prevail. The values of youth are arrived at from a reactionary stance and such a stance seldom brings good balance.

EDUCATIONAL REFORM

A system of educational process at the college level was developed in our country around the turn of the century. This system included such things as majors and minors in subject-matter fields, required courses in a core curriculum, fine-arts requirements of liberal education, language requirements at least for the B.A. degree, a system of written and oral examinations for graduate level degrees, etc. If we examine the rationales of college and university programs around the country today, we are painfully aware that these anachronistic implementations of education are still very much with us in virtually pure and unchanged forms although there is a current movement to "deschool" society. While everything else has changed with such enormity as to leave us breathless, the educational system that undergirds (or is supposed to) life remains virtually the same.

If there were no other reason for student unrest, this should be enough. But strangely, for students on many campuses, at least, this does not seem to be the focal point. Largely, students seem to go along with the outdated system, probably because there are many much more emotionally laden issues and inequities that are glaringly apparent to them. Since they will be at the mercy of college education only a few years, many of the students simply decide to last out the system for four years, more or less—rebellion seldom seems worth the trouble. But we may be certain that if all other glaring social inequities were solved, this need for educational reform could well be *the* burning issue, and is so even now with a minority of students on a minority of campuses.

Carol Remick[6] is probably quite correct when she says, "Students are looking for educational change and reform so that the university environment is responsive to the needs and crises of society . . . that education is not meeting the needs of society is at the core of student protest." Perhaps Ms. Remick is correct, but it is doubtful that the majority of students are seeing this evident truth. The implications of her remarks certainly are well founded—if we are able to overcome the more pressing problems, we shall ultimately have to turn our guns on the problem of educational reform. And one is tempted to feel with Ms. Remick that the peripheral problems cannot be solved without first attacking the core problem. It is more likely that the most engaging and emotionally laden of the peripheral problems will have to be ameliorated in some manner before we can *focus* on the core problem.

STUDENT SENSE OF DEPERSONALIZATION AND POWERLESSNESS

Powerlessness is closely allied to a sense of futility. George Wald[7] has said the present generation of students is the first in history to be unsure that it has a future. Can this sense of insecurity be the truly basic cause of student unrest? Probably not, although the threat of atomic annihilation certainly must enter the concern that students seem to have for an existential position—a position that says in effect that ours is the now generation. "We cannot afford to give much thought to distant objectives. We live now or we don't live at all." And that point of view forces attention on the pressing problems of social injustices as well as a style of life that emphasizes immediate enjoyment at the cost of a recantation of age-old values. "When we all get to heaven . . ." has been supplanted with "take heaven now."

One level of student unrest is definitely centered in feelings of depersonalization. The campuses have become large, student bodies unwieldingly large and cosmopolitan. At the same time, the institutions are in a financial bind that forces college administrations to resort to such things as large classes, classes taught by graduate students, objective testing, and automated record keeping. All this may be summed up in the number concept, that the student no longer feels like a person, but only that he is a number on an IBM card. Added to these depersonalizing influences is the undeniable shift in emphasis—so far as priorities are concerned—from teaching to research, from undergraduate concerns to graduate. Graduate programs are so expensive that a preponderance of the available finances are being spent on a small number of students, while the great majority of students who are paying dearly (in terms of their own time and effort and their parents' money) for a watered-down program of undergraduate education where again the large classes, substandard professors, and automated handling causes the undergraduate to feel that he is, and is being treated like, a nobody.

It is no secret that a large number of professors who love research and hate teaching are most delighted when the students go home and they can get some work done. All this causes an extreme disaffection with the quality of education the student is getting. And the worst of it is that he feels powerless—he cannot do anything about it.

IS THE GENERATION GAP CLOSING?

There are some evidences of a degree of rapprochement between the generations. The negotiations for the end of the Vietnam War (at least active American involvement) has had an effect in this direction. Further, a number of events occurring during the presidential elections of 1972 indicated that the older generation was in process of seeing, if not correcting, some of the errors of their ways, while the younger segment was in process of moving toward a more competition-based society.

Communitarianism notwithstanding, the mass of American young seem to be moving toward a cautious and partial

166

reendorsement of an American system of competition, the watchword of a free enterprise system. In an unusually comprehensive review of communal life in America, Sonya Rudikoff reveals the poignant hopes and the deep despairs of the communitarians: "Expectations of middle-class fulfillment have been both stimulated and denied, and its values demythicized, denuded, and vitiated beyond recognition until it appears to be not worth the cost; in consequence, the pioneers have invented something else. . . . Perhaps it is done in a doomed hopeless way, and each effort only increases the feeling of despair."[8] The survival and significance of communal living remain very much in doubt. The commune dwellers sorely lack a sense of the future and are notoriously transient. Under the careful scrutiny of the sharpest of today's youth, such a system seems to be losing its appeal.

In a careful study done at the University of Illinois at Urbana-Champaign,[9] using two groups of students, one group from a fraternity-sorority complex and one from a communal-type setting, it was shown that the commune dwellers do still give strong lip service to the ethic of cooperation as opposed to competition. However, in a discussion of the results of the study, the researchers wrote: "Recent turmoil on college campuses represents in part a generalized dissatisfaction with the values of the larger society. Despite the arguments for a new priority of values, the movement from an ethic of competition to one of cooperation is not easy to realize. No matter how much in idealistic terms such a movement may seem desirable, the contingencies of life in this society are such that eschewing of competition values is not generally rewarded. . . . While on the abstract level cooperation and regard for fellow man is desirable, in fact, the contingencies of the pay-off matrix are stacked against such behavior. While the verbal commitment to a sharing ethic is strongly reinforced among the college community, this is clearly not true for actual behavior." These researchers do admit, however, that the convictions of persons living in communes on or near this campus continue to revolve around such values as shared wealth, and shared responsibility. They further suggest that such values, reinforced by the commune environment, are capable of sustaining behavior which will continue to espouse cooperation as contrasted to competition.

Obviously, the facts are not all in as to which way young America will go. If the generation gap is closing, it is because both generations are changing. Such changes as are in evidence are results of thoughts set in motion by youthful rebellion. An evaluation of the pluses and the minuses of youth rebellion is not possible at this time. Optimistically, we might conclude that the rebellion has been a way station on the road from where we were to where we would like eventually to arrive.

Most of us know what we want in terms of a satisfying life, although it may vary slightly from one to the other of us and we may be at something of a loss for words with which to express it. Most of us earnestly wish the world (society) would somehow shape up, and that we could recapture a sense of meaning and purpose. For the older generation, we may suppose that most would like to make some changes in the establishment which would give assent to some of the demands of youth.

True, many of the older generation are uncertain that the demands of youth are redeeming in any sense of the word. "Just because we have been wrong about some things does not mean that they are inviolably right in their points of view," they say. "And more than that, they (youth) offer some realistic criticism of the status quo, but little constructive suggestion for setting things right. They are right—the problems of the poor and of the minority groups are appalling; and they are right—some establishment values have added to the problem. But these problems are not *just* the result of the present older generation's foolish values. They are the result of centuries of inequities and misjudgments. Now don't just tell us where we are wrong; we already know that. Help us find a way to shape things up."

We must all understand, young and old alike, that we cannot be individually independent (free) and at the same time be an effective member of society—a society which chooses collectively to set standards to live by and then enforces these standards by some system of sanctions, legal or otherwise. Freedom isn't free!

There seems to be a terrible misconception afloat in our world today. It is that the democratic process is a natural and easy one. No! It isn't true. The democratic process is *not* natural. Man is naturally selfish and self-serving; but at the same time, he very well may also be altruistic. Democratic process requires giving as well as taking. The democratic process is not easy. It takes hard work and long practice.

Chapter Fifteen
Human Rights and Human Value

The Preamble, as well as other rights documents, guarantees equal status under law and equal opportunity for all citizens. These guarantees *have not* been actualized; human dignity has accordingly been seriously curtailed.

Instead of "freedom and justice for all," ours has unquestioningly become a land of special opportunity for the rich (including those who have pulled themselves up by their own bootstraps), the well-born (socially speaking), the Caucasian white, and the American-born. Some would add the Protestant to this group of favorites; and that did seem to be a distinct advantage in the pre-1960s. Unquestionably, one's religious affiliation still affects his treatment in some specific instances; but a state of balance is being reached in this respect in most circles, although it still seems unwise to admit atheism and expect equal opportunity and treatment.

MINORITIES AND DISCRIMINATION

Racial injustices have most typically been cast in the mold of black-white differences. Integration of the races in housing and in schools has long been the chief vehicles from which political debates have been launched. The Brown decision of the 1954 Supreme Court set the stage for overcoming many barriers blocking blacks from advantages and opportunities in schooling. The Civil Rights Act of 1964 has opened new possibilities, new liberties, opportunities, and justices, especially in housing and employment. But as the years roll onward, these are seen by many, both black and white, as somewhat empty gestures.

With all the holding back via various counteractions, progress is slowly being made in bringing black and white under a similar umbrella of justice, although for the young black, especially, it is all painfully too slow.

But the black has not been the only minority group involved. Most civil rights legislation has been aimed at injustices perpetrated on the black; but as these rank injustices have at least been brought to public consciousness, the plights of other groups have surfaced—the Indians, the Latin-Americans, various second-and third-generation immigrant groups all have been recognized as deserving civil rights just as much.

INTEGRATION FOR WHAT?

In 1954, the idea of integration of schools sounded very good, quite generous to many blacks. This was what the black parent had wanted so long, to see his children have the advantages which seemed so obvious in equal opportunities in schooling. But as some notable progress was made—grudgingly by the older whites, eagerly by the younger whites—the concept of a black race integrated into a white society became anathema to certain young blacks. Equality and civil rights, offered even in good faith, have become not enough for many members of a black society who, having been ill-treated for generations, are at

172

last finding a sense of identity. And that sense of identity takes many forms. For the moderates, it is a black man amalgamated into an American society which is by definition neither black nor white. For the militant, it is the creation of a separate and equal (if not separate and superior) black society.

The phrase "Black is beautiful" has become somewhat tantamount to the concept that black people should discover and prize their own identity. The term *black power* for the moderates means the power base to find identity and destiny and to move forward in a brotherhood of all peoples to create a new world. The term *black power* for the militant means to overpower and destroy one society which has been hated and hateful, and supplant it with a new society.

Whether viewed from the moderate or militant power base, black Americans are no longer willing to wait or to receive gratefully. The black American no longer asks, he demands. The same is becoming more and more true with more and more groups. Now we have Chicano power championed by Latin-Americans; and surely there will be others both moderate and militant—as well as the somewhat ludicruous but sobering expressions of power such as "flower power" for the hippies. The base question is: Will our nation become a mosaic of separatist (hopefully peaceful) societies, or will we be able to return to the one-society ideal expressed but not implemented by our forefathers who founded a country "conceived in liberty and dedicated to the *proposition* that all men are created equal."

There is widespread belief that blacks, in particular, and minority groups, in general, are cooling off their campaigns toward human betterment for their peoples.

There is abundant evidence, however, if one looks for it, that all is not quiet on the civil-rights front. Two books of recent printing are clear indicators of a continuing seething anger and discontent among blacks. *Black Rage*,[1] written by two physicians, William H. Grier and Price M. Cobbs, issues clear warnings that politicians and citizens alike should not consider the late civil-rights legislation as the be all and end all of the matter of black oppression or of reactions, including violence. These authors wrote that black survival depends upon the blacks' development of a "healthy paranoia." The book *Choice: The Issue of Black Survival* by Samuel F. Yette[2] appeared at about the time of the Attica Prison tragedy. Yette's principal target is a technological society in which the blacks are relegated to neoslavery, in which there is no place for the black man who possesses only manual skills. His book brings stark testimony to the seething anger which resides in the black man; Yette believes that whites are gradually liquidating blacks through denying them equal opportunity at acquiring skills needed to make blacks competitive with whites.

So far as integration is concerned, the busing episodes of the early '70s yielded evidences of stalemate in the school integration issue. True, President Nixon's stance on busing accomplished some positive gains for freedom in one sense. In another sense, it is all too clear that pouring money into poor schools is not the answer to integration. The busing episodes of the '70s should tell us that *school* integration, however accomplished, will not bring about a social integration of the races. Nor will these confrontations confirm or unconfirm the desirability of social integration.

THE CONCEPT OF CIVIL DISOBEDIENCE

Doctor Martin Luther King, Jr. made famous the term *civil disobedience.* In the days of the most heated debates over integration, it became all too obvious to some black leaders that neither whites nor legislative bodies could be made to listen to the cries of the oppressed. Therewith came the nonviolent movement spearheaded with demonstrations and marches. When these demonstrations and marches were legislated against, civil disobedience was resurrected as a means of dealing with the intolerable. Civil disobedience has a long history; it has a heroic tradition. It is the rejection of one law for a conceived higher one. As Frank Stagg[3] points out, under civil disobedience, the apostle Peter refused to obey the Sanhedrin's order; under civil disobedience John Bunyan went to Bedford jail; under civil disobedience Martin Luther King, Jr. and many other blacks went to various jails. Because of civil disobedience many blacks have been murdered.

But there is no easy answer even within an honorable movement. It has become increasingly obvious that nonviolent marches can and will erupt; that they are often peopled with persons who hope for the eruption of violence, persons who plan such aberrations, and those whose aim it is to bring about violence in order to render civil disobedience noneffective. Unfortunately, the marches were often attended by unstable persons whose real purpose, far from being puristically non-violent, was purposely to raise hell.

CIVIL DISORDER AND MILITANCY

While a chief means of being heard for the moderate has been civil disobedience, the chief tool for the militant is civil disorder. "Burn, baby, burn" has become a watchword for the young militant. Civil disorder is not a black-white confrontation, at least, not necessarily. Young militant blacks reject the Uncle Toms among their moderate brothers; and their emotions, pent-up in rallies, often infused with hatred by small militant cadres, explode on the streets. Riots and burning of property are the results. Young whites rejecting the white establishment, sometimes on an economic basis, sometimes religious, often political, vent their spleens in riots not dissimilar in effect. In some cases, militant blacks and whites join forces in destructiveness. The militant cadre fans the flame, the knowledgeable core (nucleus) makes the first moves (throws the first fire bombs, etc.), and then, the unknowledgeable but willing mass gets into the act, and all hell breaks loose. As often as not, the largest number of rioters are more victims than insti-gators—they are the victims of those who spearhead the riot;

they are unwitting, if not unwilling, manipulanda of crowd psychology.

THE BACKLASH

Not all whites mean well. Many do. But even the well-meaning white, whether his efforts are made on behalf of black, Indian, Puerto Rican, or whomever, finds a stone wall of usually corporate resistance when these groups are offered honest help. The centuries of oppressive denial rear up in the minds of these people, and they seem unwilling to accept the proffered opportunity, whether it be in the form of good housing, equality in education, or employment.

When the honest efforts of reasonable men are rebuffed, either openly or in sullen and obvious disaffection, the human capacity for tractability is blunted and tempers rise. As Shoben[4] so aptly says of blacks, ". . . as Negroes grow understandably more militant and demanding, sectors of white society respond more repressively; and on the principle that violence begets violence, the social fabric is torn by an erupting mistrust and uneasiness, by an increasing crime rate, and by more frequent civil tensions of a highly upsetting and ominous kind."

CIVIL DISORDER AND POVERTY

Civil disorder is rampant in many forms and in many guises. Hatred of "whitey" for what he has done in the past is often cited by the blacks. Hatred of the establishment is often favored by the militant whites, student and nonstudent. But at the basis of most civil disorder lies the spectre and the reality of poverty for many, especially in contrast to the unimaginable riches of some others.

To the poverty-ridden ghetto-dweller the world consists of the haves and the have-nots. He feels that he has not had a proper chance to become a "have"; indeed, he sees himself as a pawn in the game perpetuated by the rich whose goal is to make the rich richer by making the poor poorer. Under this logic, the problem is not poverty so much as it is wealth, wealth which begets poverty through exploitation of poor people.

GOVERNMENT EFFORTS
TO BRING ECONOMIC BALANCE

Under the rubric of freedom, we may well question any governmental action which inhibits a person's wealth-producing behavior. Under free enterprise, ambition flourishes only because many people wish to work hard in order to make a better life for themselves. Socialism proposes commonalty and communality while the republic sponsors free enterprise and idiosyncrasy. Allowing free enterprise an unbridled reign often produces extreme wealth for a few and extreme poverty for the many. On the other hand, socialism seldom, if ever, lives up to its ideological promises.

Many efforts have been made legislatively to keep the extremities under control. Tax laws, especially income taxes, are designed with this in mind. But the affluent find and make the loopholes which still allow the extreme dichotomy between rich and poor. Government boondoggles are plentiful and very obvious—they are also usually well intentioned, although some have political overtones.

The concepts of minimum-income and negative-income taxes are now being widely proposed and even tried in pilot-study programs. There are extremes of viewpoint on all these things. There are people who still assert that a man can become anything he wants to become, if he wants it badly enough. To those ensnared in poverty, there seems to be no escape. Even if we agree that it is only a matter of motivation, we must concede that motivation is not easy to come by if you have no practice in being motivated. There is little doubt that to many of the disadvantaged, there is no way to get ahead. The rut seems too deep; and, realistically, too many of them are equipped not with a vaulting pole but with a crutch.

Welfare programs are an especially touchy issue. Many argue that so long as the government maintains a dole for the poverty-stricken, they will continue to be as they are. This is undoubtedly true of some—many people do not really want to work. The fault may not lie in them; it may lie in a society that has allowed people to become so motivated, or unmotivated as one may interpret it.

There is little doubt that various forms of welfare, and aid programs, ranging from Aid to Dependent Children, to Urban Renewal, Model Cities, and the Job Corps, will accomplish little unless the disadvantaged are taught the advantage of becoming self-supporting—free from dependence upon an indulgent government.

VALUES AND ATTAINMENT

Are the values inherent in a system that proclaims good in affluence positively related to a viable dignity for man? Are the values inherent in a system that proclaims good in self-support within a life style one chooses for oneself conducive to a type of freedom that man could enjoy? Perhaps in the nature of man there are some answers to the question of what types of values produce the most viable and satisfying types and expressions of freedom and dignity for the human being.

If we claim that self-support is a value to be adopted, then we shall need to include in any effort we make toward engendering this quality in modern man some elements of education which will cause him to want to continue in his self-supporting way once he has attained it. For this reason, education in the values of self-support must accompany any legislative mechanism that attempts to initiate it.

If a man, woman, child, probationer, felon, or any person at all, is to *feel* pride, self-esteem, and a sense of dignity, that person shall need tutoring in the development of that feeling. Haim Ginott[5] lucidly makes this point in dealing with the small child in the schoolroom. We must make him feel his dignity and worth; we must not cajole, reassure, or foolishly encourage him; rather, we must let him find his self-esteem in his own capacity to do, to accomplish things for himself.

It is vastly important to have the developing child, and the child becoming a man to feel the dignity that is invested in accomplishment. This is the chief failing of many of the programs and techniques growing out of behaviorism which makes it possible to train the mentally retarded child to tie his shoes, the mental patient to make his bed, and the unemployed person to take and perform a job. These accomplishments in and of themselves are good; but if the person simply does these things because he is reinforced or bribed by extrinsic rewards, then what happens to his dignity of accomplishment? No, it is summarily not enough to get people to do things for the sake of the doing; rather, we must educate them not only toward the accomplishment but toward the *pride* of accomplishment. Only in this way can we move toward human dignity and away from mechanical control.

Does there seem to be any hope? Yes and no! That there have been notable strides forward is undebatable. That there is a geometric progression of internal strife in our country together with a fast-climbing crime rate cannot be validly doubted. What we need is a break! A change in generations may pull it off eventually. The trouble is that the tactics and the thinking exhibited by the youth, understandably impatient, harbor about as many inconsistencies as do the often assinine and inconsistent points of view of their elders. No, we don't just need a break; we need a series of breaks. Perhaps a drastic change in foreign policy, a new and viable social-welfare approach, a revival of the force of love (through some viable although unpredictable means), a personality of unusual acumen in the White House—any or all these would certainly be welcomed. Why not hope? Despair will never accomplish anything!

But surely beyond the factor of hope, intelligent and energetic men and women will implement those hopes as they earnestly work, calmly solicit help and cooperation; and taking all salient factors into consideration, attempt to work the magic of motivation in the life styles of their fellows.

Chapter Sixteen
Political and Economic Impacts on Human Worth

Kenneth Kenniston[1] writes, "In the next decade of this century, Americans will be called upon to choose between three fundamentally different options concerning the future course of our society: whether to turn the clock back so as to re-create a bygone society in which our modern alienation did not yet exist, whether to 'continue' the present triumphant march of a technological process which has created these same alienations, or whether to begin to define a new vision of society whose values transcend technology." Kenniston opts for the latter.

From this statement several ideas emerge in bold relief: (1) whatever changes do occur must have their bedrock in political reform; (2) political reform will inevitably bring economic reform, for the two are inevitably interrelated; and (3) no new vision will be possible unless the mainstream of American citizens commit themselves to the proposition that new values indeed *can change* the shape and thrust of society.

Kenniston[2] argues for "Commitment, dedication, passionate concern, and care—a capacity for wholeheartedness and single-mindedness, for abandonment without fear of self-annihilation and loss of identity." I argue the same in the context of a return to a reembracing of possible human freedoms and unchallenged human dignity—such values to transcend technology cannot be achieved without a reinvestment in human dignity and, again, the bedrock of any possible change in active valuing is the political scene, which spawns economic principles, which enhance or destroy human dignity.

Protest and dissent are with us on every hand. Much of this protest is related to establishment values, some to traditional religion, much to social conditions. Still another large protest movement involves the political machine. It must be recognized, however, that dissent is overlapping, touching on many issues under a multitude of rubrics.

Loud voices are being raised, demanding an overthrow of the United States government. Many agree that drastic changes are called for in the interests of a viable democratic ideal. In service to this ideal, especially the right of free speech, we are hearing the dissent of reasonable people, of radicals, and of revolutionaries. They come from student groups, from fanatics of all ages, from subversive groups. How shall all these voices be used in the cause of freedom and human dignity? Should we seek to silence the most strident while quietly attempting to engineer political change through traditional due process?

If freedom of speech must be defended, then is repressive behavior (verbal and/or forceful) to be eternally damned? Writer William F. Buckley, admittedly a conservative, has described as "democratic indulgence" the act of walking through New York's Central Park and listening to speakers call for the downfall of the free institutions of the nation.[3] Perhaps the fundamental right of freedom of speech must be examined in the light of interpreting some such expressions as attempts at treason. Plotting to overthrow the government of the United States is criminal, and free speech seems almost paradoxically to be aiding the enemy while posing also as an inalienable right.

Must we not protest the protesters who avowedly call for an overthrow of the government!

Law and law enforcement can be repressive to freedom. As a matter of fact, freedoms and values must, in the democratic state, be expressed in such ways as to allow optimum freedom for all. As Lowe[4] states, "In our day new laws are written to ease points of social abrasion between individuals and groups with different ideals and values. . . . In this new situation, law must somehow strike a medium among different value systems, balancing the continuing desire of the individual to be free against the needs of a commonwealth which subordinates individual demands to the general welfare."

The National Commission on the Causes and Prevention of Violence, chaired by Milton S. Eisenhower, has done a commendable task in locating the causes of violence. In *The Politics of Protest,*[5] written by Jerome H. Skolnick, director of the Task Force on Violent Aspects of Protest and Confrontation, the author emphasizes the political nature of the current protest movements. The implication is that the basic attack on problems of violence in protest must occur at the political level, an attack (approach) which could make optimum use of protest movements while controlling violence.

Harvey Wheeler,[6] renowned co-author of *Fail Safe,* strikes a harmonious and optimistic note with his *The Politics of Revolution.* Wheeler feels that revolutionaries and politicians can and will be joined to gain control over the technocratic society. For him, the revolutionary spirit is a necessity if the nation is to find "a new direction and creativity in a coalition of radicals from science, technology, and politics." Jean Francois Revel[7] has, writing from the perspective of a Frenchman living in France, suggested that such a revolution could only take place in the United States.

ALL IS NOT RIGHT WITH AMERICAN POLITICS

The problems with American politics from national to local levels center to a large extent around a fast inclination toward oligarchical form in which the few govern the many. The name of the political game has become money, and the money that is absolutely necessary for the modern political campaign must come from a relatively few wealthy individuals or vested interests. We are told on good authority that presidential campaigns cost 20 to 30 million dollars, that upward from a million dollars is the price for the typical governor's campaign, and half a million is not an unusual expenditure for the campaign of a would-be United States senator. We are told on good authority that the campaigns for federal-level positions in 1972 cost over 400 million dollars.[8] When the amount of money it takes to get elected far outstrips the salary for the elected position, it is time to think seriously about who is in control of American politics. Only at county and precinct levels is it logical that the money *could possibly* come from campaign contributions given freely without vested interests.

This is not to say, of course, that there are not sizable campaign funds given by persons who have no axes to grind. It is not to say that there are no elected officials who gain election on honest money. Indeed, there are examples of persons being elected largely because they operated on minimum campaign funds; sometimes, however, exposing the opposition as catering to vested interests. That this type of claim against political opposition has become a political gambit is neither evidence of the honesty of the one so claiming nor of dishonesty of the one against whom such allegations are hurled.

American citizens must at least be aware that all is not right in politics when such vast amounts of money are, in fact, required to secure the election of most candidates. The candidates ultimately elected are not unquestionably corrupt; but it is difficult to believe that a candidate can be free from the pressure groups who financed his campaign—free to represent the majority of the people who elected him through the exercise of voter franchise. Pure motives unmixed with any degree of evil are rare indeed in politics. It is unlikely that the public will ever know the facts surrounding the Watergate incident that surfaced during the 1972 presidential campaign, for instance.

NOMINATIONS FOR OFFICE

Under our system, the people have their say at the polls. And even under some antiquated systems of vote counting such as the electoral college, this say is all-important. The fault with the system is not primarily at the election level, but at the nomination level. Too often the voter has no real choice—he is forced to choose perhaps between two evils, between two not-so-desirable candidates nominated by the major parties. The electorate has a feeling of loss of control over their own lives, and are experiencing a sense of deception which widens the credibility gap.

Nominations for most elective jobs are engineered behind the scenes, often years in advance. The vested interests that engineer the nominations all have axes to grind—they often spend their money foolishly, but never without purpose. At the gubernatorial level, the chief behind-the-scenes puppeteers are power companies, labor unions, mining interests, oil companies, insurance companies, and race-track interests. The forces that are applied to the elected official who accepts tainted campaign money are not necessarily detrimental to the people of the states, but it is foolish for the average citizen to think that he has much to say about who is nominated for what.

THE INDUSTRIAL-MILITARY COMPLEX

In his farewell address in 1961, President Eisenhower warned the American people about the growing industrial-military complex. According to Stagg,[9] there were 721 retired colonels and generals of the army and captains and admirals of the navy in the top eighty-eight industries holding contracts with the Department of Defense in 1959. Ten years later, the number of retired military officers holding office in industry had risen to

2,072 among the top ninety-five industries who held defense contracts. There is no evidence of substantial change in this trend. This becomes especially alarming when one realizes that 90 percent of these contracts are not awarded on competitive bids, but by negotiation.

The people of the United States have long been wary of a military state. But it is obvious that we have militarism functioning within the political realm of our free-enterprise system. And when one thinks that militarism of this type still feeds on our involvement in Southeast Asia, as well as what seem necessary defense systems, it is easy to see why President Eisenhower issued the warning.

The illegal release of the Pentagon papers and the prosecution of various military personnel for My Lai-type incidents have brought a vast social malaise especially to lower-class segments of the electorate who, in general, felt that Lieutenant Calley should not have even been brought to trial.

People, in general, are beginning to feel like pawns in a game being played with rules drawn up by a military state or a corporate state as envisioned by Charles Reich.[10]

FOCUSING ON THE COURTS

The judicial arm of our political system is perhaps one of the finest in the world. Even so, there are serious implications in this system for the thwarting of freedom for many, especially the underprivileged. The laws of the land often are more designed to remove the poor from the public's line of vision than to remove the causes of poverty. Witness the widespread practice of the loan shark who, in many states, enjoys almost free rein.

It is difficult to document unjust court action wherein the poor and noninfluential are given the severest penalty under due process while the affluent and influential are excused with mild hand slappings. But even where trial by jury is in evidence, the final arbiter in sentencing often is the judge. There is at least a strong invitation for judges to exercise prejudicial options in sentencing. We should be surprised if, under our present system of law, justice really can prevail; for no man, judge, clergyman, or candlestick maker, can be free from prejudice. Just laws would not entice the poor to break them. But to be poor is too often tantamount to being forced to break laws. Anatole France sarcastically remarked, "The law, in all its majestic equality, forbids the rich as well as the poor to sleep under bridges on rainy nights, to beg on the streets and to steal bread." From the poacher of the ancient feudal state to the nocturnal visitors of the trash bins in quest of the crumbs from the rich man's table, the poor are coerced to break the law; and, in these respects, the rich never would, nor ever would, need to do so. It is difficult to suggest a cure for all these ills, but let us not be unaware.

The Supreme Court of the United States under Chief Justice Earl Warren undertook to give to the accused a strong basis for asserting his rights. Some have said critically that the balance was weighed heavily in favor of the criminal and that these court decrees served to make more criminals. Perhaps so. The intent of the Warren court was probably well founded. The accused was given his rights to speak or not to speak, to gain the services of an attorney, etc. Wire-tapping was largely forbidden under this court. Under Chief Justice Burger, no clear trend in this respect is yet seen. The implications seem in a direction of a pendulum swinging back to a more balanced position.

Any attempt to balance out the good versus the bad as touching on these expressions of the rights of the accused would be sterile debate. We do know that crime has increased enormously. We do not know whether stiffer penalties and opportunities for more heavy-handedness on the part of law enforcement personnel would result in fewer and less serious crimes.

A few years hence we shall probably be able to comment more intelligently on these issues. The trend is definitely away from the softer touch inherent in the Warren court's decisions.

The no-knock legislation and a return to some other more forceful alternatives may be seen as a necessity for balancing the scales so that the criminal will not be unduly insulated from the due process of law. It may be that we are trading on freedoms— the law-abiding citizen may have more only if the accused or the suspect have less.

IMPROVED POLITICAL STRUCTURES

When the above-mentioned inequities are observed in American politics, one may not be so adamant in condemning the revolutionary who wishes to start over and build a new political system from scratch. The trouble is that the majority of the revolutionaries seem to have no viable plan, goal, or project in mind. They would simply destroy with little or no concept of what may be rebuilt to take the place of what we have.

True, some espouse the political philosophies of Mao Tse Tung, Che Chevara, Soviet Communists, and others. But evidence is plentiful that they do not really even know what these political philosophies entail. Most revolutionaries don't even know how to run a revolution!

As trite as it may sound, the basic thing that the average citizen may do is to get involved and vote. First, of course, he must register. When we consider that the majority of yippie revolutionaries—the people who are finding the most wrong with the system—are quite young, it is shocking to find that a full 40 percent of this age group (twenty-one to twenty-five) did not even bother to register to vote before the voting age was lowered. Certainly the majority never vote. The 40 percent under twenty-five who did not register compares with 26 percent of overall voting age who did not register to vote. Only about 20 percent of eligible voters over 35 did not register.

The youth vote of the 1972 campaign has presented some puzzlements as well as some causes for optimism. The youth did not vote as a block, and that in itself may indicate that these young people are not easily influenced by any particular style of political rhetoric. Of greater import is the purported size of the youth vote and the tremendous efforts made to secure both maximum registration and maximum votes. To date, the youth vote lends credence to the hope that a more aware and a more concerned new wave of citizens are entering American political affairs.

Voting seems the least any American could do to stake a claim of responsibility in government. But voting is, at best, a debatably effective act; and that fact may account, in part, for the lack of interest among disaffected youth. Why vote when our vote doesn't gain us anything, any citizen may reasonably ask.

The answer is that voting must be only the beginning. Realistically, the exercise of the vote, in and of itself, can do much to control political futures in the primaries. And that is where it all starts. Beyond that, the vote can be quite effective in deciding local issues. Blacks have raised their voting number up to 300 percent in some Southern states. If citizens do not exercise this right in the primaries, then the politicians will gladly choose the candidates.

But the proposition that most candidates are chosen behind the scenes, unfortunately, still stands. So, an aroused citizenry will have to get involved in politics at the precinct level and upwards as far as their individual influence may be expected to count. The trouble is that most of us have been silent, lazy cowards.

There are really only three ways to look at the future of politics in the United States: (1) let the revolutionaries decry and destroy what we have and hope against intelligent foresight that something better will rise from the ruins; (2) continue in the status quo and allow the government to continue largely in the hands of moneyed interests who hold no ill will against the free enterprise system (a government controlled by vested interests is better than the chaos of political revolution); or (3) shake the silent majority out of their doldrums and, with such an aroused citizenry, place political determination in the hands of the people. This last certainly includes the willingness of people from all walks of life to seek public office. In the name of freedom, which oligarchy clearly denies in many ways, we may reasonably hope that the crisis in American politics may be met with concerted and sensible action.

ECONOMICS AND FREEDOM AND DIGNITY

Economic welfare is obviously sharply related to both politics and human dignity. How can a man experience a feeling of dignity when his family is hungry and being forced into a position as second-class citizens? True, he may *have* dignity as a function of being human, he may rise up against an oppressive economic system, assert himself, and gain his place in society as a dignified person confirmed by his own economic status, his fellows, and his sense of wholeness within the system. But for many, the rut is too deep; there is viably no way out!

There is no easy way of summarizing the economic quagmires of our present day. There is no easy suggestion as to where the answers lie. So-called experts in macroeconomics have failed miserably to provide the answers.

It is easy to fix blame. Some fix blame on the Keynesian doctrines, keyed as they are to the insights of John Maynard Keynes, who, during the great depression of the 1930s, suggested high levels of government spending with spiraling national debts as the way out of the economic chaos of the depression years. These policies seemed to work miracles, and Keynesian macroeconomists were able to shake off the pleas of monetarists who claimed that such policies of deficit spending would bring chaos, eventually, along with a debt passed on to future generations. Some said the piper would eventually have to be paid; others said no.

John Kenneth Galbraith, the renowned Harvard economist, has said all along that Keynesian economics (pump-priming through federal deficit spending) would not work. He called for a system of economic controls at least as far back as 1958 when he wrote his famous book, *The Affluent Society*.[11] He has again and again remonstrated the Keynesians.[12]

With the Nixon administration of 1968-1972, there was a return to the monetarist school led by Professor Milton Friedman. This group of macroeconomists, foregoing the extremes of the Keynesians, held firmly during the earlier part of the 1968-1972 era that deficit spending was anathema and that the economy could be managed without controls. They basically championed free enterprise and supply-and-demand factors. During these years, the nation suffered through frightening inflation and dismal recession. Eventually, during the late years, a return to deficit spending came seemingly too late to bring fiscal equilibrium. Then, dramatically, in August of 1971, controls were clamped on for three months, to be followed by a prolonged Phase II.

With the Nixon administration, controls have remained with reasonable modification. Economic controls represent a confusing issue for any viable effort to elevate human dignity. Control of the economic world in a calculated spirit of moderation, a spirit which allows maximum development of human potential while providing protection from crippling economic pressures, can have profound effects on human welfare and human dignity.

The nation now finds itself in an economic turmoil. What will work and what will not is one way to phrase the question. Another way is to ask if anything will work now with so much economic insecurity residing in the consumer.

The answers must surely lie ahead in a system and an administration of politics and economics that must rethink economic models to take into consideration such things as union politics, corporate conglomerates, new family budget practices, along with all of the current events that macroeconomics seemingly did not deal with effectively in the late '60s and early '70s.

The solution of the nation's economic disasters and the reestablishment of the human dignities which have been shaken in the past years will reside *not only* in the hands of governmental elitists. True, policy-making will be done there, but an informed and a sharply aware citizenry is necessary in order to reestablish a workable economic system. The greatest danger lies in apathy among the electorate.

Chapter Seventeen

Women's Liberation: Late and Important

Prejudice to the prejudiced is invisible. So it has been with the whites who, in reasonable honesty, have thought they were not behaving prejudicially toward blacks. Male prejudice and the prejudice of the unknowingly unliberated female toward the female has also been relatively invisible until recent movements toward women's liberation. Should we not be surprised if these movements springing upon an unsuspecting public with heavy emotionality should be devoid of extremities?

In describing the vitality of the movement, McDonald[1] says, "Certainly by the end of the nineteen sixties what looked like a movement was under way. And today the women's protest has all the characteristics of a movement: the untidiness and initial diffuseness of a movement (many voices, many groups); its own N.A.A.C.P. (NOW) and its crazies (SCUM, Society for Cutting Up Men); street-theater people and zap actions; internal conflicts over goals and strategies; quarrels between personalities; conservative, moderate, and radical divisions; and serious differences as to what constitutes an authentically feminist sexual life-style."

This comprehensive statement about the confusions of the early movement perhaps is accurate, at least to the point of the 1972 Democratic convention and the campaign of that year. As the movement heads into the middle '70s, however, there seems to be more steadiness, more levelheadedness, and a careful strategy designed to obtain for women due rights without undue stresses.

So long as women's place in society was considered solely in the light of *some* Biblical admonitions and implications, women were largely immobilized. The Genesis account of woman's being created as "an helpmeet," the Apostle Paul's admonition that women should "subject themselves to their husbands," and the attendant "love, honor, and *obey*" indigenous to most religious marriage vows, all have played a part in the delayed reaction of women to their unliberated state.

But, even with the concepts of "helpmeet," subjection, and obedience, women have, for several centuries, exhibited pockets of resistance.

The level of subjugation of women implied and enforced by modern society was not so severe even in some context of bygone societies. Indeed, the Christian movement during the first century lent status to women that had been sorely lacking in some other cultures at the same and subsequent times. In England, Mary Wollstonecraft's book, *A Vindication of the Rights of Woman*, published in 1792, testified to the sensitivity on the part of some women that all women were being treated unjustly because of their sex and possibly because of Biblical references.

In America, during the nineteenth century, women's rights were relegated to the concept of women's suffrage being interpreted as the right to vote. This suffrage, realized finally in 1920, was really a compromise between the male and the female. The militant female wanted much more than just the right to vote. It must be seen as something of an assent to the incongruous that from the time when Christ spoke and acted in women's defense in the first century to the "generosity" of women's suffrage in the twentieth century, that progress in women's status had been so ponderously slow.

WOMEN'S RIGHTS AND CIVIL RIGHTS

The assertion of women's rights in the 1960s followed on the heels of successful (on the surface) civil rights for minority groups. Many women actively worked to gain civil-rights legislation; and it was a natural step for them to move for women's rights. The early leaders of the women's liberation movement were (and among most activist groups, still are) women who had worked hardest for civil rights. That they were in large part unmarried females simply attests (1) that married women are too wrapped up in matters of family (which may be seen as female subjection) to have time to work in any rights movement; or (2) that the unmarried women (who really want marriage) turn their venom upon a male world that has passed them by; or (3) that the unmarried females (who say they don't want marriage) are naturally vindictive toward males—a reaction formation against anxiety provoked by feelings of not being quite normal for one reason or another. But let it be known, that since women's liberation has become popularized, married women seem as caught up in the movement as are the unmarried. The movement has largely been accepted by most knowledgeable persons as a justified and overdue commitment to *human* rights.

Mrs. Betty Friedan's popular book, *The Feminine Mystique*,[2] advised women at large (especially married women) that they were being dominated by a male society that had conned them into producing more children than they really wanted, and into lives that were being deadened by trivia. The National Organization for Women (NOW), headed by Mrs. Friedan, evolved in 1966. This group has both male and female members. While not an underground organization, it, as well as other women's rights groups, operate with an element of secrecy inasmuch as the press has been highly, even caustically, critical.

The principal direction of reform for NOW, as well as many other emerging groups, is toward an end to sex discrimination in education, politics, hiring, promotions, and salaries. That there are serious inequities, especially in salaries for women as contrasted with those for men who do exactly the same work, is scarcely debatable. This condition grew out of an era when jobs were scarce, when it was conceded that the breadwinner needed more money than a woman who was working with no one to support but herself. With less job scarcity and with improved skills on the part of women so that they are at least equal in proficiency, the discrepancies in salary hardly seem justified on any grounds.

THE FEMINISTS AS ANTIMALE

The term *feminist* has been derived under the connotation of antimale although the term is often used loosely to apply to activitists in the movement. As a militant antimale group, it is a splinter from NOW coming about through disagreement with the main membership of NOW.

These so-called feminists are not only moving in favor of women's rights, but are also downgrading the male in the process. In essence, members of this group are against marriage, although that is not a hard-and-fast rule. Some feminists are calling out for emancipation from sex; indeed, some will not tolerate sexual relationships—this, they say, makes women a toy to be used for man's pleasure, or a breeder for his flock.

Within the feminist camp, there are revolutionary groups as well as individuals with revolutionary ideas. The Women's International Terrorist from Hell Conspiracy (WITCH) is one such group. These extremists see themselves as the first guerilla fighters against women's oppression.

WOMEN SEEK IDENTITY

Woman has been long in the process of losing her identity as a person. This identity can easily be lost in the process of being a mother. That this loss of identity is not a necessity in the culturally derived role of the wife and mother is evident; that the role of wife and mother can be the *real* identity of a woman who chooses to make it so is an unavoidable fact. But because many women have been used, and because many others feel used, it may be expected that many, if not most, women will react to a strongly worded statement originating in a feminist group—react positively, that is.

Saint Thomas Aquinas said, ". . . a female is something deficient and by chance." If women allow, through default, such an image as this to be a common evaluation, then their rights will, indeed, be lost.

Black Representative (Dem., N.Y.) Shirley Chisholm, also the first black woman presidential candidate, has said, "Of the two handicaps, being black is much less of a drawback than being female. . . . That there is prejudice against woman is an idea that still strikes nearly all men—and I am afraid most women—as bizarre." The Redstocking Manifesto (a militant New York-based group) states: "Women are an oppressed class. Our oppression is total, affecting every facet of our lives. We are exploited as sex objects, breeders, domestic servants, and cheap labor. We are considered inferior beings whose only purpose is to enhance men's lives. . . ."

Once most women derive a reasonable vision of what has happened to them, they are, at least, sympathetic, often distinctively reactive. That the crusade for women's rights *must be* waged at the expense of the male is debatable. Most males understand the feelings of women and are ready to react helpfully. Most married males understand that a liberated wife is much more likely to be an exciting wife—much more conducive to what he wants in a truly alert, vivacious, totally female female.

DOUBLE STANDARDS AND SINGLE IDENTITIES

Woman has long groveled under the concept of a double standard for sexual behavior—one, more permissive for men, and one, truly restrictive, for women. The reason behind it all was, of course, that it was the woman who had to pay the price of promiscuity—men didn't get pregnant. Now that a woman rarely gets pregnant unless she wants to, the basis for the double standard is gone. But the fact still remains that women and men *are* different. If a woman tries to throw off her shackles by emulating the conduct of man, she has restricted her freedom of being a woman having a truly feminine identity—she has just become a little-more-soft, a little-more-rounded male prototype. There seems little to be desired for either sex in this.

Woman should seek liberation for anything and from everything which prohibits her being a truly distinctive biological person. This does not make her more masculine—it should make her less so. She must cast off some time-honored shackles, but she must consider the consequences of taking on any aspect of identity that is not supportive of her biology or of her culturally derived distinctives—keeping in mind that some culturally derived distinctives can be changed. The militant invective of a minority of biological females who do not have the psychological prerogatives of being both biologically and emotionally feminine may sadly distort the thinking of some fed-up-with-the-system women who could make men very happy to be men while being more than happy with themselves as women.

Far from having it made, women do enjoy (or at least, can enjoy) some terrific benefits from their femininity. Few women would wish to rob any man of his psychological manhood. Most women relish being distinctively female.

There is, in reality, no longer a double standard in sexual freedom. Should women take this as an advantage to be exploited toward promiscuity? Would such promiscuity become freedom, or would it become enslavement? This will become the most soul-searching of all the implications for the new liberation of women.

Sex with one man for life can be a pretty restricting thing—especially if the wife suspects that she is not the only women in her husband's sex life. The realities of new sexual freedoms for women must be weighed against the possibilities of enslavement in response to the invitation for freedom. The question is inevitably wrapped up in moral and ethical considerations. Not only does it cut across legalized and religious teachings, it cuts across the deep-running rules of logic as well.

It is probable that this question must be raised in two perspectives—promiscuous sex before and after marriage. Here again, the question is fraught with moral implications. Promiscuous sex before marriage (let's assume, for argument's sake, that it isn't wrong) could become an excuse for a continuation of promiscious sex after marriage. With this as a guideline, a woman could achieve liberation before marriage only at the expense of having her marriage fail later.

Few are ready to believe that marriages can last with acknowledged sexual promiscuity within the marriage plan. Perhaps this is correct only for a transitional stage (in terms of emerging values). But one cannot help question whether or not extramarital sex would be conducive to an optimum relationship, or to well-ordered family life. True, the O'Neills would be quick to say this is ridiculous.[3] Only time will reveal how well open marriages which allow extramarital sex will work.

There is now afloat a supposedly logically conceived plan for a dual type of marriage—a plan which takes into account (1) the reality of the new morality; (2) the nature of man and woman to want to procreate; and (3) the need for family, especially on the part of growing children. It goes something like this (and has been championed by several anthropologists): persons who are physically attracted to each other should have trial marriages with the attendant joys of sex perhaps confined, perhaps unconfined, to the one-to-one relationship. Then, when love blossoms and the two wish to become parents, they would enter a new relationship which could be solemnized by a new marriage vow or may be initiated by securing a license from a state agency for having a child. With this last commitment, the parents would continue the relationship with family loyalties (still with possible extramarital experiences), so long as the growing child needs the benefits of family.

Could it work? Probably not; but then, we do need some viable plan for (1) keeping explicit sex in a privacy context, since most of us believe young children may be hurt by public display of sexual acts, (2) population control, and (3) a mentally healthy climate for child rearing. True, the Biblical plan (New Testament) of one man for one woman for life seems a defendable ideal. Sadly, it hasn't been working very well. But maybe it can be made to work and ultimately will be found to be the most viable plan after all.

ABORTION, FREEDOM, AND COMMON SENSE

In no arena of human life has a legalized, moralized, and ethically oriented concept undergone such fast changes as has abortion. One cannot speculate what was going on in the minds of people but, on the surface, a value change has swung on a pendulum with a terribly long rod, making a vastly encompassing sweep across the lives of men as it has moved from right to left. Over a four-year period, this pendulum has swung valuewise from thinking of the fertilized egg as a living organism whose willful demise by anyone at all constituted murder to the thinking that a fetus has no right to live unless so decided by the mother upon whose body the fetus is feeding parasitically.

Women's liberation forces have generally agreed that abortion laws should be removed, allowing women to assert their rights to control their own bodies. It seems altogether illogical that women's groups—even such extremists as those who chained themselves to their seats in the gallery of the parliament of Canada, shrieking their demands for control of their own bodies—could really change the stances of legislative bodies, most of which consisted of males. In the end, at least in one state, abortion laws have been liberalized to the point that any woman may have an abortion with impunity (from manmade law) on her sole initiative so long as the term of pregnancy is twenty-four weeks or less.

It is too astounding a change to properly assess. Was it a victory of women's-rights agitators over legislative bodies? Was it a victory of the American Medical Association over legislative bodies? Or was it a combined victory of women's rights and medical forces over the Catholic church?

From whencesoever came the pressures for such change, abortion laws have been liberalized, seemingly in opposition to long-standing codes of legality and morality in at least one state. There is strong evidence that others will follow. What will it mean?

Will it mean a victory for population control? Certainly it will help that cause. Will it give women control of their bodies with impunity? Yes and no. Many will have their abortions, and will suffer mental breakdowns from guilt because they have been taught that abortion is wrong. What will it mean to the normal fiber of the nation and of the world? With liberalized abortion it becomes more conceivable that deformed babies may also be destroyed, that the elderly may be destroyed when they reach certain stages of helplessness. There is no doubt that liberalized abortion involves extremely complex issues. On the one hand, the causes of dignity could be served by a careful and intelligent approach; on the other hand, decisions and laws precipitated by a rebellious stance toward long-standing cultural attitudes could damage the dignity of the human being.

Women's rights were conceived as an issue designed to improve and increase viable freedoms for women and, hopefully, to make life better for all than it had been before. It would be surprising if the extremities of a fast-paced women's rights movement did not produce some miscalculations which, later, will have to be rescinded, revised, or otherwise rectified. The cause of freedom and dignity definitely cannot be served at the expense of special groups.

The fundamental question about abortion is whether or not the fetus has rights that are violated by abortion. This, again, is a value judgment—one which has undergone tremendous overt change in a short period of time. Under existing law, the fetus has no rights—it cannot inherit, cannot exercise any of the civil rights said to be due a living human being. The consensus of the proponents of abortion (under the twenty-four-weeks gestation period), then, is that this fetus is not a living human being, for it has no capacity to maintain itself—it could not survive except as a parasite. The newborn child could not survive either, but it is no longer a parasite.

NEW MOVEMENTS AND NEW MAGAZINES

There can be no doubt that women's rights represent the most talked-about and written-about topic of the early '70s. A host of new magazines for women representing varying points along a scale from antimale to more-feminine-but-more-distinctively liberated have arrived. These include *MS.,* literary pioneer in consumer publications; *New Woman,* elegant and relevant; *Essence,* representing the black women's movement; *You;* and *Up From Under,* noncommercial and run totally by lower-middle-class women.

And now, from Beverly Hills and Jacquie Davison, comes word of a new organization, HOW (Happiness of Womanhood), which deplores the traps into which these women believe American womanhood has fallen in pressing for the equal-rights amendment, passed by overwhelming majorities of both Houses of the Congress in 1972. Mrs. Davison vows to weld the 44 million homemakers into a political force to oppose the ERA (Equal Rights Act), which must be ratified by thirty-eight states in order to become law.

In the meantime, Germaine Greer, author of *The Female Eunuch,* and Norman Mailer, male retaliator and author of *Prisoner of Sex,* carry out their disagreements in various ways, through various media. And Gloria Steinem, personable editor of *MS.,* continues on her lecture tours, leaving behind her in each city a cadre of committed who, mainly through the medium of rap sessions, press forward to relieve the inequity of a centuries-old, male-dominated society.

THE CONSOLIDATION PERIOD

Women's liberation, as a movement, seems to be more or less quietly consolidating the gains achieved. There do seem to be two distinct spearheads of the movement. One, of course, is political. Women are alert and moving in the area of female equities in political positions. This goal is a distant one, one which will take many years to achieve.

The other pressure point is in equality of educational opportunity. Here, again, inequities against women have been largely invisible because no one really took the time to look. But women's groups are looking now; and the lack of status of women in the world of education is a glaring thing. The Equal Rights Act is designed to insure that "equality of rights under the law shall not be denied or abridged . . . on account of sex by any governmental action—state or federal." The Higher Education Act of 1972 seems designed to make more specific the broader intent of the ERA. The National Organization for Women (NOW) had drawn up An Affirmative Action Plan for Equal Educational Opportunity for Women to be presented to the Department of Health, Education and Welfare.[4]

The National Education Association, at its meeting during the Thanksgiving holidays, adopted the format of a new approach in elementary education designed "to reduce the negative effects of sex-role stereotypes foisted on little boys and girls by society from the playpen on."

Ms. Steinem, editor of *MS.*, is quoted as saying, "We realized we can never be free until we rid our society of these castes."[5] Among the nonsexist materials presented to the first Sex-Role Stereotype Conference of the NEA meeting at Warrenton, Virginia, was a recording, produced by the Ms. Foundation called "Free To Be You and Me," starring such celebrities as Carol Channing, Tom Smothers, Harry Belafonte, and Marlo Thomas. Strong objections are already coming in on this project since many knowledgeable persons believe that differential sex-role stereotypes are necessary for proper sexual development. Most do agree that changes in sex-role stereotypes are

IN SUMMARY

No man can claim freedom and dignity so long as any human is denied inalienable rights. Any social movements that give women a stronger place of integrity among men without unduly impairing the rights and freedom of either is one which belongs under the banner of freedom and dignity. In its perceptible, and most far-reaching implications, a sane approach to women's rights can add immeasurably to human dignity. We must place confidence in man's ability to govern his own fate, to bring about changes that will ultimately serve him best, and to negate changes that do not prove to accomplish that which was hoped.

Chapter Eighteen
The Compelling Dignity of Human Life and Love

Life is the all-pervasive element from which the concept of human dignity emerges. Being is itself the melody to which all concerns of human life are attuned. The human search within the human situation is for life—more meaningful, more abundant life. Philosophers in the past have approached the awesome meaning of life, some allowing their queries to force closure on the proposition of being in the now, others searching behind the curtain of temporal being, on toward the quest for Being Itself or of the Being behind human being.

THE AFFIRMATION OF LIFE

Human dignity has meaning only in an affirmation of the supremacy of human life, either in the now or in the forevermore. At whichever level of meaning for life one attempts to effect closure, he moves with the depth of the search into areas of thought and of *feeling* which, being largely beyond the process of rational thought, become somewhat mystical.

As we think and feel along the corridor of concern for life, we find our energies more and more sharply focused upon the question of human dignity and of human freedom. One of the most soul-searching quandaries of the modern day is euthanasia and, more specifically, the right of the individual to *choose* his own death. It comes so trippingly off our tongues, "A person should have the right to choose to die with dignity." Such a statement is fraught with belief in both human freedom (intentionality) and of dignity.

In the context of euthanasia and of abortion, we become enthralled and, perhaps, a little frightened with the complexity of it all. Being dedicated to the proposition that human dignity has its roots firmly embedded in the issues of life, the reverence for life, and the enhancement of life, we are forced to concede that life, per se, is not the only consideration involved in the dignity question.

It would be much simpler if we could only maintain that life is all we must defend in our struggle for dignity. But when we consider euthanasia and abortion we realize that we are moving into concepts of *quality*. Is there a quality of human life that even the living thereof confronts the dignity question? The person doomed to a short life of intense pain with attendant incapacity to live with even a vestige of meaningfulness would probably say that to die in dignity is more elevating than to live in denigrating limbo. The woman who has within her body a parasitic embryo might well say that her conscious dignity is of greater profundity than is the possible loss of human dignity that may come if she seeks dissolution of that life which, in terms of the value judgment of another, abides within her.

The proposition of life does indeed bring compelling convictions about dignity. In this context, Hamlet's "To be or not to be, that is the question" takes on new meaning. And since life is the inevitable question, we shall be forced to take a fresh look at ways in which we are affirming or disaffirming life. We can become so swept up in the immediate, provoking, and demanding question of female liberation, for instance, that we fail to see that human dignity is being endangered by an easy, and possibly increasingly calloused, approach to the question of abortion. Granted, the real and clearly debatable question is where life begins, but we are in danger of failing to discern the closeness of the issue of abortion to the dignity of man. Indeed, any abortion that is performed (intentionally permitted) without careful confrontation and closure with the question of where life begins, represents a person (society) alienated from the main issue—the intentional dissolution of a human life strikes close to the heart of the dignity question.

After careful closure on the issue of where life begins, and after taking into consideration *all* salient factors, many abortions may confirm human dignity.

If we cannot see and act upon this proposition that human dignity and human life are compellingly, although complexly, related, then we are not affirming the concept of human dignity, and the persons who are attacking human dignity are winning the battle because of our default. The struggle for human dignity will demand of us a total commitment to make decisions intelligently and with much soul-searching.

LOVING AND BEING LOVED

There have been many efforts in the last few years to belittle the love ethic via experiments designed to show that so-called love is no more than a subtle expression of selfish physiological or psychological needs. Indeed, love *is* need fulfillment. As Montagu[1] says, "Love satisfies the most important of all needs: the need for love." Most such experiments have utilized rats and monkeys and have, in a measure and after a fashion, shown that love, especially maternal love, is linked to transient hormonal changes in the female. On the other hand, the Harlows,[2] working experimentally with baby monkeys, have brought some refreshing and, perhaps, unexpected revelations on the nature of love. The gist of their findings is that monkeys reared without the overt trappings of love—closeness to the mother, bodily contact, etc.—became distraught and disturbed, never able to achieve adequate adjustment, having been robbed of these tactile elements.

Psychological experiments on human love have been scant. Love of human for human is a very special thing. In the context of the fulfillment of the need for love, man could hardly be fulfilled by being loved by his dog or the radishes in the garden. Granted that the dog love example may be a tenable proposition and the radish love example is an insult to intelligence, it still remains a sharply incisive truth that human love is necessary for humans.

The subject of human love is a difficult one to research inasmuch as the concept means so many things to so many people in so many situations. Psychological experiments, to date, may have brought more heat than light. I, for one, would not like to be guilty of passing off this topic lightly on the one hand, or of presenting love in a manner typical of the high sentimentality and romanticism of the starry-eyed poetic approach, or the cloying, saccharine format of at least some of the literature emanating from organized religious communities. This does not mean that I disagree with these sentimentalities; in fact, my romantic and religious nature leads me inexorably toward this type of excess.

The point is that I believe that one cannot compose a manuscript which is dedicated to the proposition of man's dignity without getting involved in the concept of human love. I prefer to get involved, for it is my conviction that nothing so dignifies the human person as to love and to be loved.

Enough has been said in previous chapters concerning the loneliness of man in his essential existence. He is his own project and he can never escape himself. Enough has been said, too, concerning the possibilities of personal freedom being confirmed and enhanced by the presence and support of others. In short, freedom *is* (exists) in the solitary confrontation of man with himself; but freedom is enhanced, while existential loneliness is made tolerable, through encounter with others, which aids in the formation of social identity. And, paradoxically, as Bonner[3] insists, giving oneself to another in love both limits one's self-affirmation and enhances his self-actualization inasmuch as "the realization of one's inner life can be achieved only through communication and relatedness to another."

Any single example of one person loving another can be seen, in part, as exploitation and manipulation of that other. Any living relationship in which two people share things and each other's person hardly permits manipulation and exploitation to vanish. But this should not hinder our understanding that this same love encounter is fraught with elements of care, responsibility, and sacrifice for the other. Indeed, honest care and earnest seeking to become fully aware of the essence of another, the eager grasping after a union with the innermost core of another represents an unconditional belief in the sanctity of the human being.

It would be, at best, only a partial victory if we could persuade the entire world that a given person has (possesses) dignity. For a person to possess this ephemeral quality as a function of the human condition, or as a gift of God, is a happy assertion. But the proof of human dignity is surely in that one person of dignity is able to validate, to reach out toward, to affirm, to confess the dignity of another human being. Whether conjugal, fraternal, or platonic, such a confirmation of the other in an attitude we shall call love is the highest possible testimonial of the reality of dignity. R.F. Gale[4] expresses this beautifully: "Each dignifies the other by sharing with him or her a precious self, a human being in the process of becoming. Each rescues the other from the indignity of anonymity by personalizing him through accentuating self-identity and personal validation."

Erich Fromm[5] brings reality into sharp focus thusly: "Love is an active power in man; a power which breaks through the walls which separate man from his fellow men, which unite him with others; love makes him overcome the sense of isolation and separateness, yet permits him to be himself, to retain his integrity. In love the paradox occurs that two beings become one and yet remain two. . . ."

And how could we overlook Saint Paul and the thirteenth chapter of his book addressed to the church at Corinth. "Love," he said, "bears all things, believes all things, hopes all things, endures all things."[6] Jesus made love the aim of his followers when he said, "By this shall all men know that ye are my disciples, if ye have love one to another." And again, "Greater love hath no man than this, that a man lay down his life for his friends."[7] This last is seemingly a precursory and prophetic statement introducing the central theme of the Christ event, that Jesus' death (in the Christian tradition) did so dramatically dignify man in that God was willing to sacrifice his son in order that this assertion of love should remain forever with man as the most supreme of all testimonials to his worth and dignity.

LOVE AND EMOTION

Nothing so enslaves a person as being afraid of one' own self, one's own impulses and emotions. Over and over, I hear from the recorded voices of my clients in counseling and psychotherapy: "I just can't turn loose and really express the way I feel. I wish I could put my arms around her . . . I just wish I could turn loose and cry—but I just can't."

So much of life is feeling! What a loss to the world that people must go about their dreary tasks with apathy, without a smile, without a joyous note in their voices or a spritely tempo in their movements. Through our television and news-media encounters with the Chinese, we come away depressed by their seeming malaise while paradoxically and quizzically impressed with their quiet and hopefully happy resoluteness.

The schizophrenic is described as flattened, without affect; the existential wanderer is afflicted with malaise. The self, under stress, throws up a screen, the person becomes a prisoner with the shrunken boundaries of his selfhood comprising walls; and, unlike the prisoner of Chillon, these walls do a prison make. The person is shut off, a victim of his own fears, especially fears of his own emotions. The psychological self can grow only with the food of experience, especially experience indigenous to the interhuman enterprise. Without human encounter there is no will to venture, to explore, to create, to become.

And then enters love! How many times have you seen it happen? In seeing an apathetic young person turned on by love for another, even if it later turns out to be puppy love, I have marveled time after time.

In my own life, I have marveled at the power of love to rescue me from myself. Before conjugal love came to me, I was an empty shell; and then, I became turned on to life, really up; and though I was sometimes down again, love has rescued me again and again. This description given in terms of conjugal love applies with less drama to fraternal love and, for many, even more dramatically with what some describe as the love of Christ, as satori, or as nirvana—the breaking through and uniting of the person with the Ground of His Being.

Former priest, James Kavanaugh extols in beautiful prose the love between man and woman: " The world has no meaning except for love. The world is only a framework in which man can love woman and woman can love man. It is only a garden which offers them a million different backgrounds to experience their love. It gives meaning to pain, to blood, to work, even to death. Without it there is no meaning, only the emptiness of symbols and pointless monuments."[8]

LOVE AND SEXUALITY

Revolutions are typically destructive. It is an open question as to whether the sexual revolution is likely to be more destructive than redeeming. There seem to be some elements of both growth and crippling in the present situation.

Time was when sex was a hush-hush affair. It was little improved by marriage vows. For centuries, people have been in the process of denying their sexual selves, and the neuroses which have grown from this repression were likely scarcely touched in the thinking of Freud and Fenichel.

But that is all over now! Or is it? The sexual revolution has brought a type of freedom, true. However, even if we ascribe full positive value to the revolution, we shall, for a long time, be seeing the spectre of guilt extant in the lives of many, young and old alike.

Any reasonable analysis of the good and the bad of the sexual revolution must be deferred until some of the certain repercussions can be viewed in retrospect. It is understandable that overreaction is bringing a ballooning effect, which, at present, may be written off as all bad. The report on the President's Commission on Obscenity and Pornography was based on semiscientific evidence, and it might be argued on quasi-scientific evidence. The recommendations, even if accurate, may result in a heightened storm wreaking vast destruction before the clean-up stage may begin. It is unquestionably common sense that pornographic materials should, by the suggestion of the commission, be withheld from children. It is unquestionably ridiculous for intelligent persons to think that such material *can be* allowed for adults *and* withheld from children.

That the flood of prurient-interest material (especially films) is heightening the amount and joys of sexual expression, at least for a time, is not often questioned. That the same material may be highly manipulative and exploitative, especially of the female, has not escaped the attention of the women's liberationists. As Anselma Dell'Olio[9] says in *MS.*, "The sexual revolution wasn't our war." The female seems more the goat than ever of a male-sponsored revolution.

So far as women are concerned, the broader reality seems that women have been liberated by the sexual revolution. This depends, of course, on how *revolution* and *liberated* are defined.

The research of Masters and Johnson[10] has brought some startling new information to stand in opposition against earlier repressive notions concerning the orgasmic potential in women. These findings, demonstrating as they do that women have much greater orgasmic possibility than had earlier been thought, should help eradicate the concept of the frigid woman.

Then, too, in the context of swinging, it has been found that women, in contrast to men, choose to continue this type of adventure even when their husbands prefer to withdraw from it. All in all, the sexual revolution may result in demonstrating that the female is more sexual (can sustain more sexual behavior) than the male.

The revolution, in this sense, has liberated the female to expect and to enjoy orgasm. The female (we are told by researchers) is having more sex in all manners of outlets, from masturbation to lesbian cunnilingus. It may be that male-female relationship, in and out of marriage, in a general way, will be threatened by this, at least for a time. It is difficult to argue against more freedom of sexual expression for the female or the attendant balance in amount of sexual activity incumbent in this freedom. We can be sure that there will be problems of relationships arising from a larger freedom in sex for women. These problems will likely be individual and relational in terms of given one-to-one relationships.

A reasonable estimate of the effects of the sexual revolution could leave the following impressions: (1) the revolution has changed previously described perversions into acceptable practices; (2) it has resulted in removing sexual hang-ups, among the married, although the freedom-versus-guilt factor is indeterminate; (3) it has sanctioned premarital sex—many youth seem to have solved their sex problems, although illegitimacies and venereal diseases are still spiraling upward; and (4) the threshold of eroticism has been raised. With this last, one may wonder if the concept of expanded joy in sex can be perpetuated by revolutionary spirit and technique.

On the theme of love, the sexual revolution has several repercussions. In the main, young people are staying with the concept of one lover at a time, for a time. In the face of the persuasive elements of the revolution toward promiscuity, this is seen by some as a good sign. Group sex and swinging seem more prevalent among couples who have been married for a few years and who have outlived the honeymoon spirit. The revolution may expose new dimensions of love—the religious idea of one man for one woman in a relationship of conjugal love may vanish. The distinction between conjugal love and a yet-to-be-defined love relationship between and among the sexes very well could disintegrate.

Humans are sexual beings. They have denied that for too long. Perhaps it was necessary to have a revolution in order to break down the walls of restraint built by a puritanical and Victorian sex ethic. It seems safe to say that, in the interest of the person who reaches out to maturity and to self-actualization, sex must be recognized and confessed as a deep, emotionally laden aspect of life. One may well argue that sex without love is inevitably exploitative. Conjugal love without sex is unthinkable. Hopefully, the storm of extremes will pass and we shall enter a period in which sexual experience as an expression of love, totally healthy and growth-producing, will come. Such a time may see a great many changes in culture, in family life, in the marriage relationship. One cannot know just what changes will come. One can be optimistic and believe that with time the revolution will bring about a return to a sensible, love-oriented sexuality. The result of the revolution may comprise a vast improvement over the prerevolutionary repression of sex. Human sexuality has the possibility of becoming an experience for man which strongly supports his dignity. Above all, we should pose the hope and the expectation that a new sexuality will emerge, enhancing human dignity while affording a largess of joy and freedom for any two or more people who, in a love relationship, are seeking and giving fulfillment to the other(s).

SEX AND THE ISSUE OF LIFE

It would be comforting to this writer to be able to declare that sexual activities between and among persons should be indulged in a spirit of tenderness and within a context of caring about the other(s). Indeed, I do hope that this ideal can and will become largely operative in the vast majority of sexual expressions in whatever cultural framework sex behavior may be contained in evolving society.

Again, in terms of human dignity, the issues that touch closest to life itself become the crucibles in which dignity is tested. And, unavoidably, sex is one of these crucibles. Sex without love, without some measure of tenderness, of empathy, of devotion, of caring, is quite likely to become exploitative. It has been argued that sex in past generations has been repressive because of the dangers of unwanted pregnancies. It is unfortunate that this has been true. However, in the thinking of many parents, there has been an almost equal concern that promiscuous sex might negate the value and dignity of life inasmuch as the sex act is so firmly embedded within creative and procreative capability. In other words, sex is unavoidably related to the creation and affirmation of life; hence the sexual affairs of man are filled with meaning for the dignity principle.

Can a human being treat so lightly an area of life that is so loaded with meaning for human dignity as to indulge in the sex act as a capitulation to animalistic needs? Can sex relations committed only to the pleasure principle be encouraged without tarnishing the dignity of man? Will the freedom of sex without love simply return mankind to a primitivism wherein the gains in human dignity are negated?

These are the questions. The answers lie in the hearts and minds of men. The nature of human sexuality for the future should be forged from a sober reckoning with these questions. In the meantime, young bodies are caught in the cross currents of the sexual revolution. Sexual urges so powerful as to make mankind a "prisoner of sex" are maturing and being expressed. The virgin cult is dead or dying. The freedom and dignity of man is under attack. The human mind (hypothetical construct) and the human spirit (euphemism or anachronism) struggle with freedom, dignity, and reality.

DEHUMANIZATION THROUGH VIOLENCE

The increase in crimes and acts of violence, especially those against the person, is an alarming reality. One or two refreshing

215

examples of local citizenries who, through their action and concern, seemingly have turned the tides in their communities, give us some hope. It would be foolish, however, to believe that the worst is over.

Such hope is wishful thinking unless people can be aroused. Such tactics as burning serial numbers into highly salable goods, community programs on drug abuse, tipster systems that reward anonymous informers—all these things will bring good results.

The President's Commission on the Study of Violence has brought into sharp focus what many of us have believed for a long time: a major reinforcer of violence is the material shown on TV and movie screens. Violence ad infinitum, sometimes reinforced with attendant pleasant experiences, always allowing the erosion of sensitivities through overexposure, have set the pattern for imitative action and dehumanizing attitudes.

An erosion of basic morals is a part of this overall effect. It is time to call under sharp scrutiny the effects of a long-term exposure to situation ethics. Is it possible that we have allowed our acts against the person to be hidden beneath a cloak of "nothing is wrong in and of itself, it depends on the circumstances"? Isn't it, in fact, possible, even probable, that some behaviors *always* dehumanize the human? I believe that it is! We have allowed our morals to slide and have reinforced various acts against the human person to the extent that the world has become a huge "clockwork orange"; and, individually, we are in danger of becoming miniature "clockworks orange"!

Is there any hope that we may change our direction? Is there reason to hope for some type and style of moral rearmament? Of must we, as a last resort, throw ourselves on the mercies of some hopefully benevolent elitists and say, "Control us, for we cannot control ourselves"? If we do that, we shall come swiftly to the sobering quandaries posed so dramatically by Alex's prison "charles" (chaplain): "Does God want goodness or the choice of goodness? Is a man who chooses the bad perhaps in some way better than a man who has the good imposed upon him? Deep and hard questions, little 6655321." [11]

REACHING OUT FOR LOVE

Because the human person values life and has the capacity for the development of morality, he is capable of love. More than that, each person, both by nature and by cultural conditioning, needs love. If that love is not supplied, the result can be antilove, hatred, or violent behavior.

Judge Justine Polier, sixty-nine years old and a justice in New York City's Family Court for many years, explains the learning of violence from a rejection basis as follows: "A child—a human being—reaches out for love. And gets hit. And he reaches out again, and gets hit again. And he keeps reaching out, and every time he's denied. And then finally, defensively, he stops reaching. And in no longer looking for love, he loses the ability to love, and the ability to feel. The capacity to feel for another person is cut off, and he can destroy other people without reaction. And then you get rapes and robberies and murder. Take this little boy—he's tried to reach out and be loved. He's made a desperate effort. And he's been turned off. How long can you expect a child to keep reaching?"[12]

Chapter Nineteen
Positive Self-Regard and Intrinsic Worth

The pastor of my church, Reverend Deryl Fleming, prefaced a recent sermon with the following:

Whoever you are
You are not
    a brown shoe in a tuxedo world
    an odd ball or a loose end
    a dangling participle or a verb without a subject
    an also ran or a lost shoe
    a dummy or a decoy
    an expendable item or a misplaced number
    a lemon or a loser

Whoever you are
You are
    a real find
    something else
    a pearl without price
    utterly unique
    a special gift
    beauty unrealized
    a godsend

If you believe anything, believe that
No matter how you feel
God does not make worth-less persons

Reinhold Niebuhr, in his *Nature and Destiny of Man,*[1] emphasizes man's self-love as a fundamental and pervasive "sin." It seems to Niebuhr, and to many others, that man has made himself the center of his existence, thus denying God, and thus committing himself to a life of frustration, unhappiness, and anxiety. Undoubtedly the concept of self-centeredness is among the most confusing issues of living when one tries to understand the possibility and the possible implementations of man's freedom.

THE HUMANISTIC VIEWPOINT

In the conservative theological sense, the great enemies of a God-centered religion seem to be in humanism, which proposes that supreme value is invested in the human organism; in pantheism, which posits the supreme influence in nature and the laws of the universe; and in deism, which places God outside the range of human experience. Theism, by contrast, is the avowed position of most theologians; and this concept places God in a transcendental position as a person who guides the destinies of men and the universe, and who may be experienced by man through the indwelling Holy Spirit. It is in the context of theism that man's self-love has been seen as a pervasive sin.

This viewpoint, impinging upon man in the religious community, has, in many ways, often caused him to feel unworthy and unacceptable in his humanity.

It seems to many critics that conventional religion is based on the assumption that, at the very outset, none of us are any good, and that it is only as we disown our humanity that we can experience meaning and satisfaction. These critics say that the faith, as it has been delivered to untold millions of traditional Christians (at least), tends to deny life at almost every turn, to annihilate selfhood, to disclaim meaning in this present world, and to bind man to a gospel of hope focused on the eternal *future*. Under such a distortion, man could hardly become other than less self-directed, less in control of life, less free.

Ironically, it has been the existentialists and the humanists, the avowedly most despised among traditional Christian theologians, at least, who have offered to deliver man *from* this distortion of the acclaimed Christ event as well as *to* the possible acceptance of the mainline of teachings found in the Holy Scriptures. Happily, humans are being saved from such gross error by persons who themselves often do not espouse a system of conventional religiosity.

Carl Rogers and A.H. Maslow are among many who have reacted in an opposite direction from Niebuhr on the matter of self-love. Out of a background of a quarter century of psychotherapy with disturbed individuals, Rogers[2] makes this statement:

> Actually it is only the experience of a relationship in which he is loved (something very close, I believe, to the theologians' "agape") that the individual can begin to feel a dawning respect for, acceptance of, and finally, even a fondness for himself. It is as he can thus begin to sense himself as lovable and worthwhile, in spite of his mistakes, that he can begin to feel love and tenderness for others. It is thus that he can begin to realize himself and to reorganize himself and his behavior to move in the direction of becoming the

more socialized self he would like to be. I believe that only if one views individuals on the most superficial or external basis are they seen as being primarily the victims of self-love. When seen from the inside, that is far from being their disease. At least so it seems to me.

In describing the "fully functioning person," Maslow[3] says, "He will have no conditions of worth—he will experience unconditional self-regard."

SELF-ACCEPTANCE: KEY TO INTERNAL HARMONY

No person can arrive at adequate personal adjustment unless he likes himself. No person can really be free to like himself unless he is affirmed in his optimistic view of life and self by significant others. A person who likes himself will behave in such a manner as to achieve social acceptance and inner harmony.

Self-acceptance is a state of mind which must be practiced to be continually operative. Self-acceptance or self-rejection germinate with equal ease. It is important that the former be germinated rather than the latter in the early years of a child's life. The emerging self is a fragile thing. It can be seriously warped in the formative stages, however. Happily, if a positive self-regard is nourished well, it will become deep-rooted; and if it is deep-rooted, it can then withstand the rigors of many crises.

A positive self-regard can grow with proper feedback from significant others, but it must be generated in a climate of self-possibilities. Many personalities are blunted because significant others ask too much of the embryonic self. Children must be encouraged to do their best, but they should not be required to achieve beyond their reasonable limits. Failure breeds failure and success, success. True, every person should have an ideal toward which he strives, but the ideal should not be too discrepant with the real, with the attainable. Although there must be wide individual differences among persons, there is no need for crippled self-esteems. We must expect only the reasonable from ourselves and from those to whom we are significant others.

It is clear that the person who does not feel this self-regard will become more and more convinced of his depravity, more and more desperate to be relieved of guilt, more and more enslaved to the need to justify his existence. Dedication services, church work, confessions—all of these and others will be sought and utilized to assuage guilt, thus hopefully restoring personhood.[4] With all this striving, man would not have to be ashamed of being human. But, sadly, he would no longer *be* human.

OTHER POSSIBLE CAUSES OF SELF-DEVALUATION

It is likely that the critics of religion have overexposed their venom. It is obvious that feelings of inferiority and self-devaluation stem from other sources than religious asceticism. Freud's concept of the harsh superego, which could cause neurosis with constricted life styles and guilt reactions, was an open hostility to religious forces. In his concept of the drive for excellence, Adler did not seem to propose such an origin for his concept of "inferiority feelings." For Adler,[5] man's striving seemed based on a drive mechanism stemming from the helplessness of the infant.

The tendency so prevalent among men to denigrate self has proceeded from social systems of feudalism, class consciousness, and authority-based belittling of persons—even in the father-son type of relationship. What is the bedrock cause of the will to power on the part of some and the resulting feelings of inferiority and loss of self-esteem on the other? Is it human nature or human nurture? We cannot say; but we may feel quite strongly that the authoritative parent, the human devaluing process of some styles of religion, and political systems which have subjugated the common herd are all ramifications of whatever the base cause might be.

A CASE OF FALSE DICHOTOMIES

It is easy to see that many great thinkers have placed the matter of self-regard into dichotomies or into segmented conceptual systems. Thus foolish and selfish pride occupies a firmly rooted position as a damnable human trait, while a selfless service with self-denial and love of God and others seems to be seen as most redeemeing. For many thinkers, there are no in-betweens where one may have self-love and, at the same time, be other-oriented or, in a basic religious context, God-loving. But the matter of self-regard surely is like almost all other concepts—a matter of continuum where pretentious self-worship is, indeed, for many, at the low point, while concern for others lies at the other end of the continuum. But, even here, we have to be careful, for we must logically realize that the high point does not exclude positive self-regard but, rather demands it. Any reasonable examination of the first two of the Judaic ten commandments, especially as paraphrased by Christ, must result in such a conclusion. "The second is like unto it . . . thou shalt love thy neighbor *as* thyself." How can there possibly be that much separation of God, self, and neighbors as is implied in some theological teachings?

In her book *The Virtue of Selfishness*, Ayn Rand[6] sets forth a new concept of egoism. Ayn Rand and Nathaniel Branden,[7] under the label of "objectivist ethics," take a fresh new look at the logical place pride and self-esteem must take in man's valuing system if he is to survive the modern world and maintain a relatively free society. It may be that service and concern for others (altruism) will come to be seen positively *only if* it enhances self-esteem.

The objectivist ethic has done a valuable service in making many of us understand how we have become entrapped in a system of altruism. Such a system undoubtedly does benefit others, and it may well benefit the do-gooder; but there is a falsity of motive and an attendant loss of self-esteem which probably *could be* enhanced if people would just acknowledge the self-serving nature of their good deeds.

While this logical discounting of altruism appears helpful, it is not, within the purview of this writing, necessarily true that *all* altruistic service is, at its root, self-serving. If human beings, by nature, value life, are capable of outreaching love and, by nature, observe universal rules of justice (these things have received at least tentative empirical acceptance through the research of Kohlberg among others), then I feel that the dignity of the human is enhanced by holding that man may be other-directed, not solely as a condescension to his self-serving but, rather, as an expression of his true nature to reach out in love toward other human beings and *for the sake of other human beings.*

THE COSTS OF WORKING FOR SELF-ESTEEM

The person who, for whatever reason, has adopted a life style of trying to prove his worth often comes to the conclusion that he can never really achieve a feeling of worth this way. Sooner or later, he will become sick with the futility of his strivings. But having been conditioned through long years of experiences to the idea of working for credits in causes outside himself, it is not easy to unlearn old positions regardless of how wrong they may be.

As man continues to try to prove his worth, he continues to be uncreative—blind to the fact that he can never prove it. How sad! A profound realization that he has *intrinsic* worth because of nothing except his humanity, would make it possible for him to *become* a person of integrity, even though he may have failed to measure up to some arbitrary standard. Lacking this, many people have had no choice other than to discredit their heritages and to leave behind them outmoded value systems. But, in doing this, they develop a deep sense of alienation. Not being able to measure up to unrealistic expectations, they give up and cop-out.

Many people have left their churches, and have disowned what to them has become a punitive and puny God. People *have* to get out of the system which has become a mass of religious entanglements. We may judge that many of them really want back in, but will not allow themselves to return at the cost of personal integrity. Intelligent men can never ignore what they discover about themselves and about their world.

BEYOND HUMANISM—MORE FREEDOM TO CHOOSE

The humanist view of man proposes that in spite of everything and because of nothing, man is loved. He can dare to accept his being and say a monumental yes to life. He can cease his protests. He can thus make both a declaration of freedom and a commitment to self-responsibility.

Realizing that one cannot *earn* love, one can give up the enslaving focus on a law to be kept, a heaven to be gained, a hell to be shunned. One is delivered to *this life* with freedom to be an unreserved participant in the ongoingness of life now![8]

Man doesn't have to strive for acceptance; just knowing he is human is enough. He can recapture his zeal for life and live it vigorously in this confusing, contingent world. He can thus understand and embrace his own being. He can sustain his existence and he can feel good about it.

Adopting the humanist and existentialist view of life leaves man open to viable choices as to what he will consider to be the basic essence of his life. He can leave the search for meaning within the humanistic framework. On the other hand, the person with a yearning toward the supernatural explanation of life and destiny can easily reembrace a Christian faith he had been forced to abandon. Or he can adopt or readopt any other position of religious faith.

Man can *feel* saved from his sins (feelings of unworthiness, however provoked, as well as misdeeds, however conceived, in terms of whatever values); he can be saved to a new concept of his own being; he can be saved to an at-oneness to his world (a sense of identity); he can be saved to community with others—without needing to devalue his fellowmen. These same feelings of freedom could be extant within the purview of any position of faith in whatever concept of diety. Maybe this, after all, is the peace that passeth understanding!

226

Chapter Twenty
Freedom, Intrinsic Worth, and Open-Ended Living

Man emerges and grows into his authentic self as he lives each existential moment as an experience in the ongoingness of life, a moment to be cherished. But living existentially does not mean that mankind relinquishes each moment with sorrow and with dread that what has been can be no more. Life is a process and each moment is (or can be) a joyful one. But the person who is most authentic, who lives his freedom, and who, as Van Kaam[1] says, lives life and is not lived by it can accept without sorrow the good gifts of life and is ready to release them when they fade away.

Van Kaam[2] suggests that the authentic person no longer feels that it is necessary for him to see the whole road clearly before he feels free to move. As such, he learns to accept every existential moment with all risks and possibilities, for he realizes that real life can be lived only today, not yesterday or tomorrow.

We must, in the process of life, define what is desirable—this must be done in terms of what is possible at a given time and under given circumstances. True, one may hold some values absolute, but in the welter of everyday life, he must release some of his idealism in service to realities. To quote de Madariaga,[3] "Our eyes must be idealistic and our feet realistic." Our systems of value must have a measure of flexibility; but without the idealistic, our realistic surely would fall short of the possible mark.

Utopias seem to come from the seedbed of the American dream. And this is commendable, provided we realize that our utopias *are dreams.* Too much of the time we have seen our utopias not as dreams but as logical points of destination if we only take the right path, engage the religious ethic of hard work and self-denial, and if we live long enough. In this century, we have been force-fed on utopias from the Shangri-La of the filmed saga through *Walden Two,* the equally fictitious Great Society, and the present rambunctious and raucous promises of a host of politicians. As we have pursued our utopias, we have inevitably found only ourselves at the feet of these rainbows. We should be ready now to accept valuing, becoming, and utopias, not as fact, but as process. To so accept would not hamper our sense of freedom and dignity. The goals would be, and must be, to reach, not to grasp. Our reach would measure our freedom and our commitment to the search would testify to our dignity.

TOWARD EMOTIONAL MATURITY

Inevitably, any value is laden with emotional affect. We cannot commit ourselves without emotion, we cannot approximate the closing process with life without feeling. But ours should be an emotional maturity, not an emotional binge. Even in our emotional life (maturity), we must be content with process, for we are in process of becoming. Any arrival at a utopian state of emotional maturity or of achieving a world free of need and frustration would be victory but for a moment. Then our human urge for quest and novelty, being stymied, would break us; for the human animal can exist as human only if he continually strives toward goals that are attainable, yet never attained, as the end-point of his existence. His must be a state of continual arrival, arriving at one level of being, and then pressing on, within the context of a new becoming, toward a new being. Thus, in the Wedding-Existentialist viewpoint man will be, at last, in confrontation with being itself.

For the existential present we must be content with being-in-becoming—that is, the high state of a *logical* freedom, beset as we are by so many hindrances to a perfect, harmonious equanimity. Such a perfect equanimity must be our supreme value, while we hold shifting values in our constant encounter with life, with our being-in-becoming.

Sartre,[4] an atheistic existentialist, says that value is choice; he insists that not only does man *have* freedom, but that man *is* freedom. What other organism, after all, has the power to choose a value—what more profound epitome of freedom is there than this man-creature? At the same time, Sartre asserts vehemently that one cannot have freedom and be committed to a given set of values as in doctrinal religion. Such commitment robs one of his freedom.

Against this position some conventional religionists have declared that there is no freedom without bowing down to God and receiving His blessings, including the removal of guilt for sin. In her book, *The Wider Place*, Eugenia Price[5] has made this point clear. For her, true freedom comes only through subjugating oneself to Christ, who has, through his omnipotence, removed the stigma and the domination of sin from our lives. These positions are poles apart, at least at first glance. Actually, each in his own way calls for total commitment to a proposition.

Commitment to a proposition of values and to a quest that places one in process of being-in-becoming toward even more fulfilling being and possibly toward an eventual confrontation with being itself, forces the person inward to self-identity, which, on the one hand, is largely framed from externals, with interactions with significant others both on a personal confrontation basis and as a locking-in process with the ideas of others. On the other hand, this self-identity eventually begins to feed on itself—the person having thought out his own values and set his own goals is more discretely his own person. Thus he has developed an inner self in the humanistic framework or he is gaining fuel for his fires from external forces which, for some, become internal in the indwelling when viewed from a spiritual perspective. The way the individual does view this proposition is further validation of his freedom, his freedom to so view the source of his own power.

Any way it may be conceptualized, the person reaches the position of affirming and confirming himself; one commits himself to his values and goals, thus bringing about an inner strength which releases inward freedom permitting the individual to become a self by choice. In this verbosity there is a rich insight—choosing one's self and committing oneself to this choice brings about an aliveness and an eagerness to shout a monumental yes to one's existence. Routine existence is no more, the will to live is no longer an expression used medically in speaking of the physically dying; it is, rather, an expression of the highest form of virility in the most fully functioning person. Such commitment should make malaise and depression obsolescent. Yes, it is an idealistic thought; and the harsh realities of life will still depress the committed. But not for long!

Within this pattern of thought, there is a mystical element which disturbs many people. The train of thought does, indeed, bring one to the bright sunrise of a person's being for himself. It could possibly result in a mass of released and committed persons—committed to their own personhood in a world gone mad. If there is an implication that choosing one's self is, on the one hand, selfish and, on the other hand, plausible only for the extraordinary person, then we must come down from the clouds to confront the world of ordinary men and women who hopefully may direct their energies toward the creation of a better society. It must be conceded that much of the existential literature does not come back to earth, but it can be asserted that it *could*. It might be argued that if self-choosing persons committed themselves not only to their own enrichment but, having attained that, to the creation of a great society, then the prospect for a community of men in a semiutopia would be greatly enhanced.

THE PARADOX OF COMMITMENT

Within the religious, and even the political dimensions, the hue and cry is for commitment. Successful religious and political ideologies down through the ages from Islam to communism have made the same position of commitment. The same idea is carried into the world of sports—deep commitment is the only thing that will win the championship, etc. In the contest of commitment to causes, it is clearly man's first-line obligation to commit himself to embellish and find expression for his own inner nature—to accept himself as a special, significant, distinctive being of dignity and worth.

Commitment is obviously and paradoxically a loss of personal freedom. Yet, it is difficult to believe that causes may be promoted and ideologies advanced without this act of giving oneself *en toto* over to the cause.

The term *commitment* has become anathema to many if not most of our youth. Not that they agree with Sartre that commitment is the great robber of freedom. Their hostility is based on their suspicions that the commitments that have been recommended to them represent unattainable goals of idealism, narrowly conceived systems of thou-shalt-nots with religious legalisms, or personal commitment to a political system that fosters competitiveness in the extreme, is based on materialistic valuing, and places upward mobility at the apex of values. For many of the young, none of these commitments make good sense. Typically, persons caught up in materialistic valuing demonstrate an anxious preoccupation with having possessions to the end that it becomes impossible for them to enjoy life fully.

SOFT COMMITMENT VERSUS HARD COMMITMENT

Life without values is unthinkable—there would be no anchorages, and insecurity would be the certain result. A hard commitment to a system of values is just as untenable, especially when those values have been derived by authority outside oneself. If freedom is to be the central concept of a life, one can only exercise his freedom in the context of value judgments arising from his process of choice. This brings us around to the idea that one may live with values with security only if the value system recognizes the growth process. One may even be committed to an open-ended valuing process in which the individual dedicates himself to promoting a system of values in his life with concession to the possibility that his values will change from time to time as new information is fed into the system. We must have something to live for, but this something is not inevitably static; indeed, to conceive it as unchangeable is to deny progress, change, growth, and freedom.

In the act of becoming, we must have change and forward growth or we cannot have self-actualization.

How sad, the failure of conventional religion! Instead of having a religion that allows one to move forward, seeking new ways of affirming life, we have embraced commitment to a life of legalized thou-shalt-nots. Not that thou-shalt-nots are inherently bad. Not at all. The individual must be controlled both for his own good and the good of the many. But freedom, dignity, and growth must not therewith be stultified.

Our young people are finding out that the values we are being called upon to commit ourselves to in the name of high religion are neither a service to ourselves nor to the rights of others. They have, instead, been called into commitment to false values in no way related to the ten commandments, and that have no meaning in terms of man's brotherhood and man's humanity to man. The demands of commitment to such a system of values is foolishly constricting, not freedom-oriented. No wonder the young are copping-out in large numbers.

The values our young are being called upon to adopt come not from their own sense of right and wrong, but from outwardly imposed positions. One young man I knew a few years ago had a choice of jobs—either to load cases of beer onto trucks or to work in a factory making bomb casings for the Vietnam War. He chose the beer-handling job. His parents insisted that he make bombs with which to annihilate the North Vietnamese rather than make available beer, which they had identified through their own valuing process as demon rum. It was the honorable, even the patriotic, thing to do to make the bombs—or so they implied.

Bishop Sheen[6] speaks of a divorce between the Divine Gospel and the Social Gospel having become so "chasmed that today they are regarded as mutually exclusive." Not so, says the bishop. "How did we ever get into this divorce of the Divine and the Secular? He who truly loves God cannot do so without loving his neighbor."

CONFORMITY AND INDIVIDUAL FREEDOM

Tillich says, "The individual can be free without destroying the group." He visualizes a "conformity which is based on the free activity of every individual." Conformity is clearly not necessarily a loss of freedom. It is so only when we conform without objection, confirming for all time the status quo. Bugental[7] prefers the term *authenticity* as an expression of a happy admixture of things as they are and as they logically could be—"we are authentic to that degree to which we are at one with the whole of being (world); we are authentic to the extent that we are in conflict with the givenness of being."

Whatever else we may say about commitment and values, we must surely recognize that we are living in a world of changing values.

One could perhaps hope that emerging new values are nearer to the original rules laid down in the ten commandments than have been the interim distortions which have allowed us to live in the throes of prejudice, bigotry, and renunciation of the integrity of the individual human. It may be that man is making many bumbling mistakes on his way back to new and realistic sensitivities toward his fellowman, and it may be that he is moving grossly in the wrong direction; it is hardly debatable that values are in transition. We can hope that his movement will bring about both renewed freedoms and new freedoms.

Some transition-makers are extreme, of course. Explorers and pioneers always are. The hippies and communitarians are widely condemned, but they are conducting radical experiments in new ways of living and loving. They have broken sharply with the establishment. Jourard[8] suggests that they may become our teachers, pointing the way to a better way of life than we have been enduring under our false, competitive system.

THE INTERNAL LOCATION OF A SENSE OF WORTH

In pointing out the nature of the person who has been through successful psychotherapy, Rogers[9] states, "The renewed person is content to be a process rather than a product. He feels furthermore that the only proper source of values lies within himself. Less and less does he look to others for approval and disapproval; for standards to live by; for decisions and choices."

A person who has been made to feel free from the pressure of forces and values outside himself has an internal location for his sense of worth. Not that he devalues others. Indeed, just the opposite. He accepts others, affirms them in *their own* valuing process. He is more tolerant of others' views.

The person who has been awakened to his freedom and dignity does not expect to find his personal meaning and fulfillment apart from himself, in the "out there" of others, causes, crusades, material possessions, or vocational callings. He does not have to bargain with people for his sense of worth and esteem. His living consists not in his being a receptacle, a cistern; but in his being a *wellspring*, a source of life!

The free person knows that he is received. He has come to accept himself as a legitimate human being and is beginning to abandon his efforts to justify his existence. He no longer has to prove his worth, nor does he have to *belittle* his life. He is conscious of the fact that in the midst of his unique life struggles he is being sustained, and from this he seems able to infer that he is accepted, received, loved, and affirmed in this universe.[10]

The person who is able to accept himself as legitimate will abandon his efforts to justify his existence, for he is already worthy. There seem to be two basic types of human beings. The one is working in order to prove his worth, to pay his debt for what he has been made to believe is his inherent worthlessness. The other feels received and sustained in the knowledge that to be human is to have assured for himself a place of special importance in this universe.

This latter type is living the open-ended life. He is happy with an open-ended life always moving toward a greater achievement, but knowing that his acceptance is not conditioned on achieving.

Many years ago, the poet Oliver Wendell Holmes,[11] in describing an insignificant seashell dweller, wrote words which now seem fresher than the dew of a new morning:

> Build thee more stately mansions, O my soul,
>> As the swift seasons roll!
>> Leave thy low-vaulted past!
> Let each new temple, nobler than the last,
> Shut thee from heaven with a dome more vast,
>> Till thou at length art free,
> Leaving thine outgrown shell by life's unresting sea!

Notes

NOTES AND REFERENCES FOR CHAPTER ONE

1. Skinner, B. F. *Beyond Freedom and Dignity,* New York: Alfred A. Knopf, 1971.

2. Lamont, Corliss. *The Philosophy of Humanism,* Fifth Edition. New York: Frederick Ungar Publishing Company, 1965.

3. Rollo May, the most renowned of modern classical humanists is best known for two books, *Love and Will* (1969) and *Power and Innocence* (1972), both published in New York by W. W. Norton.

4. Skinner, B. F. *Beyond Freedom and Dignity,* New York: Alfred A. Knopf, 1971.

5. Abraham Maslow was the most prolific and revered of humanists, sometimes referred to as the father of the new humanism, the third force in psychology. He has written many books, chief among which

is probably *Toward a Psychology of Being.* New York: D. Van
Nostrand Company, Inc., 1962.

6. Excerpt from Shostrom, Everett and Kavanaugh, James. *Between Man
   and Woman.* Los Angeles: Nash Publishing, 1971.

7. Ibid.

NOTES AND REFERENCES FOR CHAPTER TWO

1. Skinner, B. F. *Beyond Freedom and Dignity.* New York: Alfred A.
   Knopf, 1971.

2. Skinner, B. F. *Walden Two.* New York: Macmillan Co., 1948.

3. As given in an address at the Center for the Study of Democratic
   Institutions, Santa Barbara, California and published in *The Center
   Magazine,* Volume V, Number 2, March/April, 1972. Toynbee,
   Arnold. *Beyond Freedom and Dignity,* "An Uneasy Feeling of
   Unreality."

4. Skinner, B. F. *Beyond Freedom and Dignity.* New York: Alfred A.
   Knopf, 1971.

5. From an address given by Chaim Perelman at the Center for the Study
   of Democratic Institutions, Santa Barbara, California in January
   1972.

6. Wheeler, Harvey. From an article in *The Center Magazine.* January/
   February, 1972.

7. From an address given by Lord Ritchie-Calder at the Center for the
   Study of Democratic Institutions, Santa Barbara, California in
   January, 1972.

8. Skinner, B. F. "I Have Been Misunderstood. . . ." *The Center
   Magazine.* March/April, 1972.

9. Skinner, B. F. *Beyond Freedom and Dignity.* New York: Alfred A.
   Knopf, 1971.

10. Platt, John. "A Revolutionary Manifesto." *The Center Magazine.* March/April, 1972.

11. Black, Max. "A Disservice to All." *The Center Magazine.* March/April, 1972.

12. Ibid.

13. Klineberg, Otto. *Social Psychology.* New York: Holt, Rinehart and Winston, Inc., 1954.

14. Kohlberg, Lawrence. "The Development of Moral Character and Ideology," In M. Hoffman, ed., *Review of Child Psychology.* New York: Russell Sage Foundation, 1964.

15. Ibid.

16. Rest, J. "Developmental Hierarchy in Preference and Comprehension of Moral Judgment." Unpublished dissertation, University of Chicago, 1968.

17. Kohlberg, Lawrence and Turiel, E. *Research in Moral Development: The Cognitive-Developmental Approach.* New York: Holt, Rinehart, and Winston, 1971.

18. Ibid.

19. Chomsky, Noam. "The Formal Nature of Language." *Biological Foundations of Language.* E. Lenneberg, editor. New York: John Wiley, 1967.

NOTES AND REFERENCES FOR CHAPTER THREE

1. London, Perry. "The End of Ideology in Behavior Modification." *The American Psychologist.* Volume 27, Number 10, October 1972.

2. White, R. W. "Motivation Reconsidered: The Concept of Competence," *Psychological Review.* Volume 66, 1959.

3. Olds, J. and Milner, P. "Positive Reinforcement Produced by

Electrical Stimulation of Septal Area and Other Regions of Rat Brain." *Journal of Comparative and Physiological Psychology.* Volume 47, 1954.

4. Etzioni, A. "Basic Human Needs, Alienation and Inauthenticity." *American Sociological Review,* Volume 33, 1968.

5. Skinner, B. F. *Beyond Freedom and Dignity.* New York: Alfred A. Knopf, 1971.

6. Smith, M. Brewster. "Three Psychologists and How They Grew." *Psychology Today.* September, 1972. Dr. Smith's autobiographical sketch is one among three included here.

7. Kohlberg, Lawrence. "The Development of Moral Character and Ideology," *Review of Child Psychology.* M. Hoffman, editor. New York: Russell Sage Foundation.

8. Sampson, Edward E. *Social Psychology and Contemporary Society.* New York: John Wiley and Sons Inc., 1971.

NOTES AND REFERENCES FOR CHAPTER FOUR

1. Whyte, William H. *The Organization Man.* New York: Simon and Schuster, 1956.

2. Skinner, B. F. *Beyond Freedom and Dignity.* New York: Alfred A. Knopf, 1971.

3. Jourard, Sidney M. *Disclosing Man to Himself.* Princeton: D. Van Nostrand Company, Inc., 1968.

4. Dostoyevsky, Fyodor. *The Brothers Karamazov.* New York: Heritage Press, 1960.

5. Rogers, Carl R. *On Becoming a Person.* Boston: Houghton Mifflin, 1961.

6. Dostoyevsky, Fyodor. *Notes from the Underground.* As translated by Constance Garnett. New York: Dell Publishing Company, 1960.

7. Rand, Ayn. *The Romantic Manifesto*. New York: The World Publishing Company, 1962.

8. Eron, Leonard D., Huesman, L. Rowell, Lefkowitz, Monroe M., and Walder, Leopold O. "Does Television Cause Aggression?" *The American Psychologist*. Volume 27, Number 4, April 1972.

NOTES AND REFERENCES FOR CHAPTER FIVE

1. Jourard, Sidney M. *Disclosing Man to Himself.* Princeton: D. Van Nostrand Company, Inc., 1968.

2. Tillich, Paul. *The Courage To Be.* New Haven, London: Yale University Press, 1952.

3. Ibid.

4. Frankel, Marvin. "Morality in Psychotherapy." *Readings in Psychology Today.* Del Mar, California: Communications/Research/Machines, Inc., 1969.

5. Mowrer, O. Hobart. *The New Group Therapy.* New York: D. Van Nostrand, Inc., 1964.

6. Rogers, Carl R. *Client-Centered Therapy.* Boston: Houghton Mifflin Company, 1951.

NOTES AND REFERENCES FOR CHAPTER SIX

1. Dostoyevsky, Fyodor. *Notes From the Underground.* As translated by Constance Garnett. New York: Dell Publishing Company, 1960.

2. Skinner, B. F. *Beyond Freedom and Dignity.* New York: Alfred A. Knopf, 1971.

3. Sartre, Jean-Paul. *Existentialism and Human Emotions.* New York: Philosophical Library, Inc. 1957.

4. Madariaga, Salvador de. *Portrait of a Man Standing.* University of Alabama: University of Alabama Press, 1968.

5. Hallie, Philip B. *Restless Adventure.* Roger L. Shinn, ed. New York: Charles Scribner's Sons, 1968.

6. Sartre, Jean-Paul. *Being and Nothingness.* New York: Philosophical Library, 1956.

7. Oppenheimer, R. From a paper appearing in *The American Psychologist,* Volume 11, 1956.

NOTES AND REFERENCES FOR CHAPTER SEVEN

1. May, Rollo. *Psychology and the Human Dilemma.* Princeton: D. Van Nostrand Company, Inc., 1967.

2. Ibid.

3. Phillips, J. B. *Your God Is Too Small.* New York: Macmillan, 1958.

4. Maslow, Abraham. *Toward a Psychology of Being.* Princeton: D. Van Nostrand Company, 1962.

5. Dostoyevsky, Fyodor. *Notes From the Underground.* As translated by Constance Garnett. New York: Dell Publishing Company, 1960.

NOTES AND REFERENCES FOR CHAPTER EIGHT

1. Sartre, Jean Paul. *Being and Nothingness.* New York: The Philosophical Library, 1956.

2. Frankl, Viktor E. *The Doctor and the Soul.* New York: Alfred A. Knopf, 1960.

3. Cox, Harvey. *The Secular City.* New York: The Macmillan Company, 1965.

NOTES AND REFERENCES FOR CHAPTER NINE

1. Skinner, B. F. *Beyond Freedon amd Dignity.* New York: Alfred A. Knopf, 1971.

2. May, Rollo. *Psychology and the Human Dilemma.* Princeton: D. Van Nostrand Company, Inc., 1967.

3. Mowrer, O. Hobart. *Learning Theory and Personality Dynamics*. New York: Ronald Press, 1950.

4. Kenniston, Kenneth. *The Uncommitted*. New York: Harcourt, Brace and World, 1960.

5. Frankl, Viktor E. *Man's Search For Meaning*. New York: Washington Square Press, Inc., 1963.

6. Kenniston, Kenneth. *The Uncommitted*. New York: Harcourt, Brace and World, 1960.

7. Kavanaugh, James. *A Modern Priest Looks At His Outdated Church*. New York: Trident Press, 1967.

8. Reisman, D. *The Lonely Crowd*. New Haven: Yale University Press, 1961.

9. Fromm, Erich. *Man For Himself*. New York: Holt, Rinehart, and Winston, Inc., 1947.

10. Glasser, W. *The Identity Society*. New York: Harper and Row, 1972.

11. Erikson, Erik. *Identity, Youth, and Crisis*. New York: W.W. Norton, 1968.

12. May, Rollo. *Psychology and the Human Dilemma*. Princeton: D. Van Nostrand Company, Inc., 1967.

13. Miller, Arthur. *Death of a Salesman*. New York: The Viking Press, 1949.

14. Tillich, Paul. *The Courage To Be*. New Haven: Yale University Press, 1952.

15. Tournier, Paul. *The Meaning of Persons*. New York: Harper, 1957.

NOTES AND REFERENCES FOR CHAPTER TEN

1. Rogers, Carl R. *On Becoming a Person*. Boston: Houghton Mifflin Company, 1961.

2. Maslow, Abraham. *Toward a Psychology of Being.* Princeton: D. Van Nostrand Company, Inc., 1962.

3. Rogers, Carl R. *On Becoming a Person.* Boston: Houghton Mifflin Company, 1961.

4. Ibid.

5. Toffler, Alvin. *Future Shock.* New York: Random House, Inc., 1970.

6. Jourard, Sidney M. *Disclosing Man to Himself.* Princeton: D. Van Nostrand Company, Inc., 1968.

7. Braden, William. *The Private Sea LSD and the Search for God.* Chicago: Quadrangle Books, 1967.

8. Ibid.

9. Donne, John. From his classic, *Devotions XVII.*

10. Tyler, Leona. *The Work of the Counselor,* Second Edition. New York: Appleton-Century-Crofts, Inc., 1961.

11. Rogers, Carl R. *On Becoming a Person.* New York: Houghton Mifflin Company, 1961.

12. Cooley, C. H. *Human Nature and the Social Order.* New York: Scribner, 1902.

13. Mowrer, O. Hobart *The New Group Therapy.* Princeton: D. Van Nostrand, Inc., 1964.

NOTES AND REFERENCES FOR CHAPTER ELEVEN

1. Thoreau, Henry David. This quotation is excerpted from the classic *Walden.*

2. Moustakas, Clark E. *Loneliness.* Englewood Cliffs, N.J.: Prentice-Hall, Inc., 1961.

3. Reich, Charles A. *The Greening of America*. New York: Random House, 1970.

4. Revel, François J. *Without Marx or Jesus*. New York: Doubleday, 1971.

5. Kenniston, Kenneth. *The Uncommitted*. New York: Harcourt, Brace and World, 1960.

6. Jourard, Sidney M. *The Transparent Self*. Princeton: D. Van Nostrand Company, Inc., 1964.

7. Mowrer, O. Hobart. *The New Group Therapy*. Princeton: D. Van Nostrand Company, Inc., 1964.

8. Buber, Martin. *I and Thou*. New York: Charles Scribner's Sons, 1958.

9. Jourard, Sidney M. *Disclosing Man to Himself*. Princeton: D. Van Nostrand Company, Inc., 1968.

NOTES AND REFERENCES FOR CHAPTER TWELVE

1. Berne, Eric. *The Games People Play*. New York: Grove Press, Inc., 1964.

2. Ibid.

3. The reader should see the very readable, *I'm Okay, You're Okay*, written by Thomas A. Harris, published by Harper and Row, 1969.

4. Berne, Eric. *The Games People Play*. New York: Grove Press, Inc., 1964.

5. May, Rollo. *The Meaning of Anxiety*. New York: Ronald Press Co., 1950.

6. Branden, Nathaniel. *The Psychology of Self-Esteem*. Los Angeles: Nash Publishing Company, 1969.

7. Rogers, Carl R. *Becoming a Person*. Boston: Houghton Mifflin Company, 1961.

8. Kirkpatrick, Clifford. *The Family: As Process and Institution.* New York: Ronald Press Company, 1963.

9. Knapp, Robert H. "Changing Functions of the College Professor," in *The American College.* N. Sanford, ed. New York: John Wiley and Sons, Inc., 1962.

10. Goode, William J. "A Theory of Role Strain," *The American Sociological Review,* Volume 25, 1960.

NOTES AND REFERENCES FOR CHAPTER THIRTEEN

1. Diebold, John. "Goals to Match our Means," *The Social Impact of Cybernetics,* Charles R. Dechert ed. New York: Simon and Schuster, 1966.

2. Huxley, Julian. *New Bottle For New Wine.* New York: Harper and Brothers, 1957.

3. This statement by Werner Von Braun was reported widely in news media.

4. Madariago, Salvador de. *Portrait of a Man Standing.* University of Alabama: University of Alabama Press, 1968.

5. Skinner, B. F. *Walden Two.* New York: Macmillan Company, 1948.

6. Rand, Ayn. *The Fountainhead.* New York: Bobbs-Merrill, 1968.

7. Rand, Ayn. *Atlas Shrugged.* New York: Random House, 1957.

8. Shinn, Roger. *Tangled World.* New York: Charles Scribner's Sons, 1965.

9. Toynbee, Arnold. "Why I Dislike Western Civilization," *New York Times Magazine,* May 10, 1964.

10. Packard, Vance. *Hidden Persuaders.* New York: David McKay Co., 1957.

11. Heidegger, Martin. *Discourse On Thinking.* New York: Harper and Row, 1966.

NOTES AND REFERENCES ON CHAPTER FOURTEEN

1. Macdonald, D. Introduction. In Levine, M. L., McNamee, G. C. and Greenberg, D., eds. *The Tales of Hoffman.* New York: Bantam, 1970.

2. Reich, Charles A. *The Greening of America.* New York: Random House, 1970.

3. May, Rollo. *Power and Innocence.* New York: W. W. Norton, 1972.

4. Shoben, Edward Joseph, Jr. "The Campus Community and the Futureless Generation." *The Counseling Psychologist,* Fall, Volume 1, No. 3, 1969.

5. Ibid.

6. Remick, Carol. "A Critique." *The Counseling Psychologist,* Fall, Volume 1, No. 3, 1969.

7. Wald, George. From a speech given at the Massachusetts Institute of Technology and reproduced in *The New Yorker,* March 22, 1969.

8. Rudikoff, Sonya. "O Pioneers. Reflections on the Whole Earth People." *Commentary,* Volume 54, Number 1, July 1972.

9. Rappaport, Julian; Bernstein, Douglass A.; Hogan, Michael; Kane Jennifer; Plunk, Martha; and Sholder, Mark. "Fraternal and Communal Living: Values and Behavior on the Campus." *Journal of Counseling Psychology,* Volume 19, Number 4, July 1972.

NOTES AND REFERENCES FOR CHAPTER FIFTEEN

1. Grier, William H. and Cobbs, Price M. *Black Rage.* New York: Basic Books, 1968.

2. Yette, Samuel F. *Choice: The Issue of Black Survival In America.* New York: Putnam's Sons, Inc., 1971.

3. Stagg, Frank. "Facts about Civil Disorder." *The Baptist Program*, August, 1970.

4. Shoben, Edward Joseph, Jr. "The Campus Community and the Futureless Generation." *The Counseling Psychologist*, Fall, Volume 1, No. 3, 1969.

5. Ginnott, Haim. *Teacher and Child*. New York: Macmillan Company, 1972.

NOTES AND REFERENCES ON CHAPTER SIXTEEN

1. Kenniston, Kenneth. *The Uncommitted*. New York: Harcourt, Brace and World, 1960.

2. Ibid.

3. Buckley, William J. This remark taken from an address by Mr. Buckley made in Austin, Texas, on July 24, 1970.

4. Lowe, C. Marshall. *Value Orientations in Counseling and Psychotherapy*. San Francisco: Chandler Publishing Company, 1969.

5. Skolnick, Jerome H. *The Politics of Protest*. New York: Ballantine Books, 1969.

6. Wheeler, Harvey. *The Politics of Revolution*. Berkeley: The Glendessary Press, 1971.

7. Revel, Francois. *Without Marx or Jesus*. New York: Doubleday, 1971.

8. See *Time* magazine, October 23, 1972.

9. Stagg, Frank. "Facts about Civil Disorder." *The Baptist Program*, August, 1970.

10. Reich, Charles. *The Greening of America*. New York: Random House, 1970.

11. Galbraith, John. *The Affluent Society*. Boston: Houghton Mifflin, 1958.

12. Galbraith, John. *The New Industrial State.* Boston: Houghton Mifflin, 1971.

NOTES AND REFERENCES FOR CHAPTER SEVENTEEN

1. McDonald, Donald, "The Liberation of Women." *The Center Magazine.* Volume V., No. 3, May/June 1972.

2. Friedan, Betty. *The Feminine Mystique.* New York: Dell Books, 1970.

3. O'Neill, Nena and O'Neill, George. *Open Marriage.* New York: M. Evans and Company, Inc., 1972.

4. Scott, Ann. "It's Time for Equal Education," *MS.,* October 1972.

5. This comment by Ms. Steinem was included in a news release about the 1972 NEA convention.

NOTES AND REFERENCES FOR CHAPTER EIGHTEEN

1. Montagu, Ashley. "Love," in Albert Deutsch, ed. *The Encyclopedia of Mental Health: Volume III.* New York: Franklin Watts, 1963.

2. Harlow, Harry F. and Harlow, Margaret K. "The Effect of Rearing Conditions on Behavior." *Bulletin of the Menninger Clinic,* No. 5. 1962.

3. Bonner, Hubert. *On Being Mindful of Man.* Boston: Houghton Mifflin, 1965.

4. Gale, R. F. *Developmental Behavior: A Humanistic Approach.* London: Macmillan Company, Collier-Macmillan Limited, 1969.

5. Fromm, Erich. *The Art of Loving.* New York: Harper and Row, 1962.

6. Apostle Paul. *The Holy Bible,* I Corinthians, Chapter 13, verse 7. New American Standard Bible, 1960.

7. Christ comforts his disciples in *The Holy Bible*, St. John, Chapter 13, verse 35 and Chapter 15, verse 13, King James Version.

8. From the last chapter of *Between Man and Woman*. Los Angeles: Nash Publishing Company, 1971.

9. Dell'Olio, Anselma. "The Sexual Revolution Wasn't Our War," *MS.*, Spring, 1972.

10. Masters, William H. and Johnson, Virginia E. *Human Sexual Response*. Boston, Little, 1966.

11. Burgess, Anthony. *A Clockwork Orange*. New York: W. W. Norton and Company, Inc., 1963.

12. These comments, made by Judge Justine Wise Polier, were taken from an article, "The War Against Children," by James Mills in *Life Magazine*, May 19, 1972.

NOTES AND REFERENCES FOR CHAPTER NINETEEN

1. Niebuhr, Reinhold. *Nature and Destiny of Man*. New York: Scribner, 1949.

2. Rogers, Carl R. "Niebuhr On the Nature of Man." *The Nature of Man in Theological and Psychological Perspective*. Simon Doniger, ed. New York: Harper and Brothers, 1962.

3. Maslow, Abraham. *Toward A Psychology of Being*. Princeton: D. Van Nostrand Company, Inc., 1962.

4. Friesen, Walt. *Letter To Herb*. Unpublished document.

5. Adler, Alfred. *Individual Psychology*. New Jersey: Littlefield, 1968.

6. Rand, Ayn. *The Virtue of Selfishness*. New York: W. W. Norton, 1965.

7. Branden, Nathaniel. *The Psychology of Self-Esteem*. Los Angeles: Nash Publishing Company, 1971.

8. I am indebted to Walt Friesen for the paraphrasing of some of his language contained in his *Letter To Herb.*

NOTES AND REFERENCES FOR CHAPTER TWENTY

1. Van Kaam. "The Goals of Psychotherapy from the Existential Point of View." Alvin R. Mahrer, ed. *The Goals of Psychotherapy.* New York: Appleton-Century-Crofts, 1967.

2. Ibid.

3. Madariaga, Salvador de. *Portrait of a Man Standing,* Alabama: University of Alabama Press, 1968.

4. Sartre, Jean Paul. *Existentialism and Human Emotions.* New York: Philosophical Library, 1957.

5. Price, Eugenia. *The Wider Place.* Grand Rapids: Zondervan, 1966.

6. Taken from Bishop Sheen's newspaper column.

7. Bugental, James F. *The Search For Authenticity.* New York: Holt, Rinehart and Winston, 1965.

8. Jourard, Sidney. *Disclosing Man To Himself.* Princeton: D. Van Nostrand Company, Inc., 1968.

9. Rogers, Carl R. *Becoming a Person.* Boston: Houghton Mifflin, 1961.

10. Friesen, Walter S. "Characteristics of a Free Person." *Omniscope.* Volume XI, No. 2, Spring 1965.

11. From *The Chambered Nautilus,* classic by Oliver Wendell Holmes.